W9-BEX-110

Frederick Beringer, co-founder (1840-1901)

Jacob Beringer, co-founder (1845-1915)

Beringer

A Napa Valley Legend

By Lorin Sorensen
with Fred Beringer

Typography
by Ellen Kirby

Silverado Publishing Company
St. Helena, California

Produced by Silverado Publishing Company,
P.O. Box 393, St. Helena, California 94574
Copyright ©1989 by Lorin Sorensen
All rights reserved.

Distributed by St. Helena Productions,
St. Helena, California

Library of Congress Catalog Card
Number 88-092709

ISBN 0-942636-03-1

First Edition

Book design by Lorin Sorensen
Typography by Ellen Kirby
Jacket front cover photo by Ed Cooper

Contributing photographers:
DeWitt Jones
Ed Cooper
Richard Wharton
Faith Echtermeyer
Mark Kauffman
Lorin Sorensen
Fred Beringer
Jennifer Lamb

Contributing writer:
James Beach Alexander

In appreciation:
*To the late Fred Abruzzini's family for providing
many of the historical photos for this book.*

Acknowledgements:
A very special thanks to the following people
who have been so helpful in providing the
information, consultation and assistance that
has made this book possible:

*Mike Moone, Tor Kenward, Bill Knox, Joan
Powers, Jim Barfield, Jim Eckert, Guy Kay, Jim
Tonjum, Janelle Thompson, Fred Abruzzini, Al
Abruzzini, Roy Raymond Sr., Ramona Beringer,
Cathy Beringer, Bob Steinhauer, Ed Sbragia, Mary
Ann Bautovich, Ed Palmer, and John York.*

Opposite: *A view of the famous
Beringer wine aging tunnels taken by a
travel magazine photographer in 1940.*

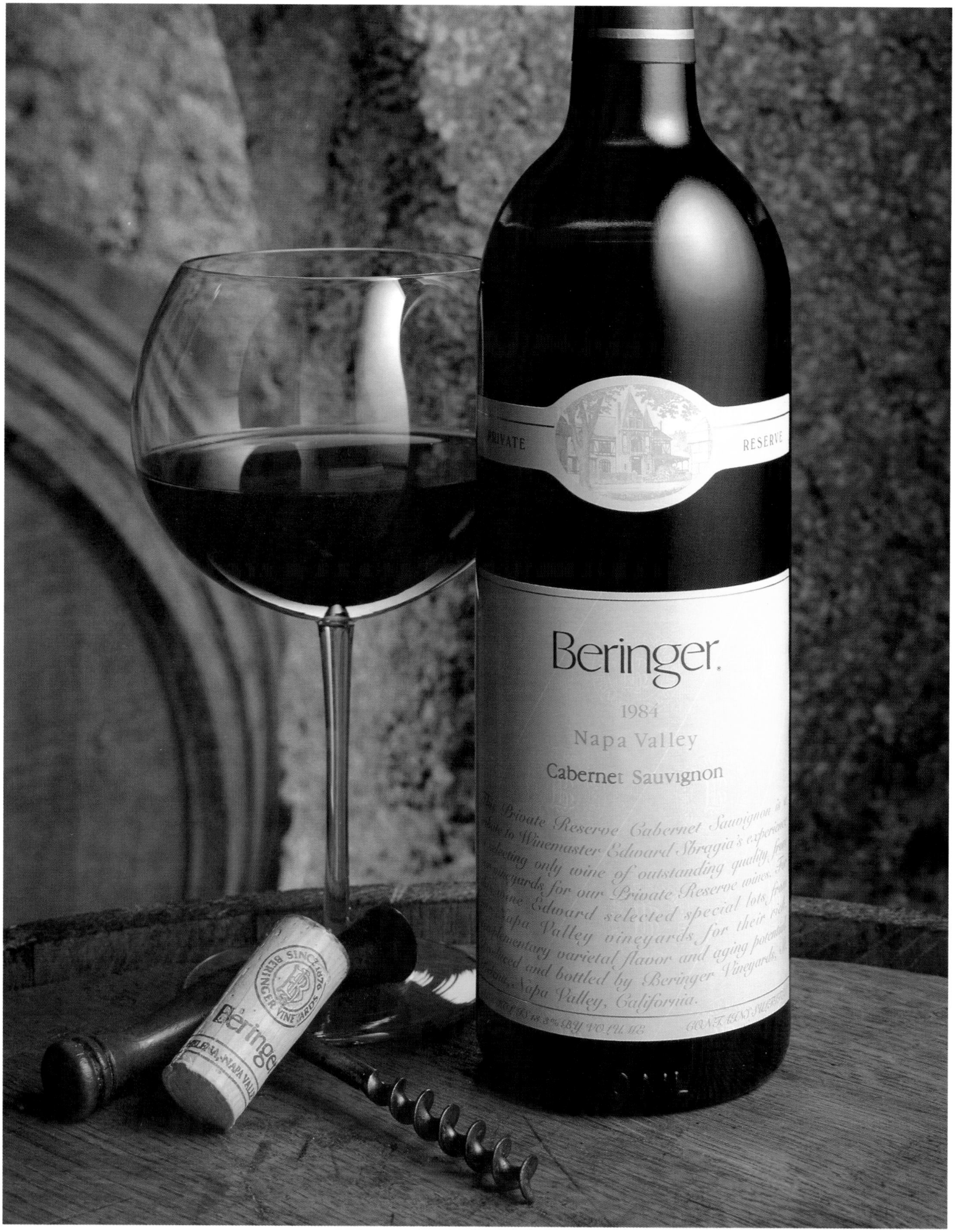
PRIVATE
RESERVE
Beringer
1984
Napa Valley
Cabernet Sauvignon
Beringer

Contents

One of the most beautiful old homes in the Napa Valley, Rhine House charms Beringer visitors with its Victorian elegance and manicured gardens.

RHINE HOUSE

Foreword

Beringer winery has seen a lot of changes in the more than one hundred years since my great-grandfather Jacob and his brother Frederick built it. But one thing that has always stayed the same is their time-honored tradition of warm hospitality.

It was a custom carried on with grace even in the hard times by my great-aunt Bertha when she managed the winery. Fred Abruzzini was a master at entertaining when he ran it, and my father Otto and uncle Roy Raymond expanded on the welcome when they first opened the Rhine House to the public. Today, the friendly people of Wine World are continuing to make Beringer the nicest place to visit in the Napa Valley.

A lot of famous personalities have stopped by. In the early days it was such business and literary figures as Andrew Carnegie and Robert Louis Stevenson. When I was growing up on the property learning the cellars and vineyards in the 50s and 60s, it was film and sports stars like Clark Gable, Max Baer, and others.

Through the years the winery has been a favorite place to visit for all kinds of people, and they always seem to come back again and again. It's more than beautiful old buildings and cool underground cellars but one of California's few historical landmarks still in operation. Needless to say, I'm very proud to have been a part of it.

So, here's to all those past and present who have helped Beringer grow better with age. And to those yet to discover its great wines and everlasting hospitality.
Cheers!

FRED BERINGER, 1989

Hospitality would become an early Beringer tradition. Jacob, left, entertains winery guests gathered at the wassail bowl in 1904.

Built in 1876, the original stone
Beringer building is the oldest
continually-operating winery in
the Napa Valley.

It's easy to make fine wine.
Just start with good grapes and
practice for a hundred years!
Beringer

NAPA VALLEY
America's most famous wine-producing region is a
patchwork of brilliant fall colors at harvest time.
Along the river on the valley floor, at the left, looking
east between Oakville and Yountville Crossroad,
grows some of Beringer's finest grapes. A section of
their Gamble Ranch vineyards can be seen at the top
of the picture above. Nearby, world-class Beringer
Cabernet Sauvignon is tended on the very land off
State Lane where George Yount planted the first
vineyard in Napa Valley 150 years ago.

WINTER MUSTARD
Wild March mustard blankets a Beringer Chardonnay vineyard along Big Ranch Road
near Napa. During the mustard season when the vines are dormant, Napa Valley is
covered with the beneficial winter flowers. They like cultivated ground best and legend is
that the first mustard seeds were brought to California by early Spanish missionaries who
scattered them to mark their trails.

By April the mustard has been mowed and the vines pruned. A Beringer worker bundles Chardonnay cuttings from which dime-size buds will be grafted onto root stock planted to start a new vineyard.

A cordon-pruned Beringer vineyard on Yountville Crossroad during the spectacular Napa Valley mustard season which occurs January through April.

SPRING FROST

Smudge pots are a familiar part of the Napa Valley scene. Set out along the borders of the vineyard during the frost season in the spring, they are lit when the temperature dips to freezing. They usually work in concert with wind machines which stir the air. Many of the vineyards now have even more effective overhead sprinkler protection. Water from the sprinklers freezes a cocoon of ice around the delicate grape buds, protecting them from damaging lower temperatures.

Morning light emblazons a section of Beringer's Gamble Ranch vineyard near Oakville.

Opposite: *State Lane Vineyard near Yountville which produces Beringer Cabernet Sauvignon. In the spring, after the dormancy period when they are pruned, the vineyards are tilled and begin leafing out again. Soon the vines will bloom and set the new crop of grapes.*

25

THE GRAPES

What makes wine made from Napa Valley grapes world-famous is the perfect combination of all the right elements, including warm days during the growing season for maturity, and cool nights for the acid necessary for quality and character. Beringer vineyardists have enhanced these natural benefits by carefully matching varietals of Cabernet, Chardonnay, Pinot Noir, and others to the best soil, terrain, and micro-climate suited to them.

A cool morning fog lifts over the Beringer vineyards in Knights Valley during harvest season. Located about 17 miles northwest of the winery, this picturesque region has its own appellation, due to its unique soil and climate, and produces prime Cabernet Sauvignon and Sauvignon Blanc.

27

FALL HARVEST

As the grape clusters mature in the warm sunny days of fall, berry samples are checked constantly for optimum ripeness that will assure another outstanding vintage. When it is time to pick, crews are brought in immediately before changing temperatures can adversely effect the desired sugar. Grapes are picked into "trays" and tossed into bins or trailers which are taken directly to the winery crusher and dumped.

Seasoned workers pick Cabernet Sauvignon from author Lorin Sorensen's vineyard along Silverado Trail in St. Helena. It is a fortunate independent grower whose grapes qualify to be made into premium Beringer wine.

Dumping just-picked Chardonnay.

THE CRUSH

Grapes are brought to the Beringer winery by truck or "gondola" trailer and dumped into a hopper where an auger carries them into a crusher which breaks the skins and separates stems and leaves. From there the "must" is pumped to the fermenting tanks before final pressing. Reds are fermented with the skins for color. Whites are usually fermented without skins.

Shoveling waste "pomace" from the crusher.

A slowly-rotating auger moves Zinfandel into the crusher.

Jacob and Frederick's old roof-top observatory looks out high above their still-active winery.

Barrel-aging Cabernet Sauvignon in the old cellar.

THE LONG REST

In tribute to the old masters, nothing has been found better than oak to impart the character necessary to finish fine Cabernet Sauvignon in the aging process. Other Beringer premium varietals are barrel-aged as well, providing one of the most eye-pleasing aspects of the winery operations.

Tiers of French oak cooperage age premium Beringer wine in the new barrel building.

THE GROWERS
*Chabot estate, near St. Helena, is typical of the independent family-owned vineyards
whose grapes bring more variety and character to Beringer wines. Situated in a unique
micro-climate, its partly terraced hillsides have produced award-winning Cabernet
Sauvignons with a distinctive rich minty flavor.*

A Beringer tractor with vertical mowing bars trims harvested vineyard rows. Removing the heavy growth will make the job easier for pruners later in the winter dormant season when the leafless canes are cut back.

Getting a Beringer truck ready for a long day's work in the vineyards.

Illluminated by the setting sun, lofty Mount St. Helena dominates the landscape at the upper end of Napa Valley. In a cabin on its slopes Robert Louis Stevenson wrote Silverado Squatters. *The legendary mountain forms an impressive backdrop for Gasser Vineyard which grows Chenin Blanc for Beringer.*

Harvested Knights Valley vines in November.

Steep grassy hillsides, oak trees dripping with Spanish moss, and cattle ranches neighbor the Beringer vineyards in rustic Knights Valley.

HOME VINEYARD
A lone wind machine for frost protection, and trellised vines, are concessions to modern viticulture, otherwise this autumn view of Beringer's Home Vineyard would be hardly changed in more than a century. Lying just over the hill behind the winery, the vineyard site was part of Jacob Beringer's original land purchase in 1875 and has been in continuous grape production since he planted it about 1880. Jacob's son, Otto, and his family lived in the farm house until the 1930s. At the right, a Beringer foreman checks the vineyard at the end of the season.

Jacob, left, and Frederick Beringer in their cellar with their trademark carved wine cask about 1885.

The Brothers

Jacob and Frederick

ONE of the great showplaces of the Napa Valley, Beringer winery has stood for over a century at St. Helena's shady north entrance where it has played host to generations of visitors while turning out some of the finest wines in the world. In the early days the famed landmark was called Los Hermanos "the brothers" for the two adventuring men who founded it, Jacob and Frederick Beringer.

They were immigrants to California, by way of New York, from Germany where both were born in the town of Mainz in the picturesque Rhine Valley. Frederick's birth was in 1840 and that of his brother Jacob in 1845. Their father Louis was in the wine business, having descended from a long line of vintners who had mastered the grape, and it was only natural that the boys would be inclined to follow family tradition. It was considered a noble endeavor for wine was part of the German diet and the most important product of Mainz. So it was here amid the hustle and bustle of the trade, the busy river barges, the sounds of laden wagons on cobble streets, the festive labor of the crush and the wonderful smells and mysterious attraction of the cool cellars that the brothers spent their formative years.

Young Frederick became more interested in the business side of winemaking than in washing barrels and shoveling pomace so, at the proper age, his parents sent him off to Paris for studies at St. Louis College.

He would remain in Paris afterward, where he worked for a few years, and then set out to see the world. His travels would eventually take him to Mexico for a time and then to New York where he settled in 1862.

Unlike his brother, Jacob Beringer enjoyed toiling in the cellars and would spend his youth in Mainz learning the wine-making and barrel-building trades. He got a job as cellarmaster at a large wine cellar in Berlin and later, at age 23, went home to Mainz where he was made cellarmaster of the prestigious J.A. Hart & Company wine cellars.

Meanwhile, across the Atlantic, Frederick's first American business experience was not in wine, but in brewing. In 1866 he became a malster, buying barley in Canada, having it malted in Buffalo, and then selling it in New York City. It was a fairly simple process in which the select barley grain was spread on a flat floor, then turned and raked periodically until it sprouted, then it was oven-baked into the malt substance used for beer-making. There were handsome profits to be made for a good businessman, especially one schooled in the old German traditions who could speak the language and knew the beverage trade.

As his malt business prospered, Frederick was soon hobnobbing with Buffalo's elite and taking part in the political life of the city. He wrote Jacob about his great success and urged him to come at once to New York state where boundless opportunities awaited. That

Young Frederick Beringer prospered in the malt business in New York after arriving from Germany in 1862. He enjoyed American politics and is pictured, right, at Niagara Falls in 1883 with two friends including Grover Cleveland, center, soon to become President of the United States.

was all the persuasion needed to lure young Jacob across the water and in the following year, 1868, he arrived by sail in New York City. His first job there would be as foreman of Truche & Winkenbach wine cellars. Within a year or so, having learned passable English, he tried his own hand at business, opening a wine shop on 10th Street where he specialized in fine German wines and seltzer waters.

But the small town life of his early background was a force too strong to keep Jacob long in the big city. The transcontinental railroad spanning the two oceans had opened a new rush for land on the Pacific Coast and excited talk among his customers about the fertile farms and lush vineyards springing up out there soon got his curiosity. Jacob had to see for himself. In 1870, he said goodbye to New York and left by train for San Francisco, there taking the Bay ferry and the new rail line up to the Napa Valley where he had heard the climate was ideal for wine grapes.

It was all he had hoped! A long narrow valley angled perfectly to catch every ray of the full day's sun, warm days and cool nights, and located inland from the sea far enough with tall mountains between to block out the cold summer fog. The soil was light and rocky on the slopes and deep and fertile on the valley floor. It reminded him in many ways of his native Rhine Valley. Others before him had thought so too.

German immigrant Charles Krug had established his vineyard and winery at St. Helena nearly a decade earlier and was already turning out some widely acclaimed wines. Several more vineyards and wine cellars were scattered among the farms the length of the verdant valley and Jacob knew that this was the place to put down his roots. Within a few weeks he would get a job with Krug as cellar superintendent, and began making his own plans.

Five years later, when the property next to Charles Krug came up for sale, he had learned much and saved enough money to make an offer. The place was a 215 acre tract of land that ran from the Napa River, along the south boundary of Krug, west across the road and into the wooded hillside to the upperwaters of York Creek. Sellers were William and Marie Daegener who had purchased the farm a few years before from the pioneer Hudson family.

The agreed price was $14,500, nearly half what the Daegeners had originally paid, and the property was

Old friends in Germany wished Jacob Beringer well in his new California wine venture. Artist Charles Fuchs sent this comic sketch from Berlin in 1878 depicting the vintner exhorting a motley mix of stereotypical Americans to help him build his winery.

ideal for what Beringer had in mind. It included a good two-story farm house and a small hillside vineyard, with plantable land clear down to the river. The house stood against the hillside in a grove of valley oaks and it was here at a slightly higher elevation that he could visualize his new winery.

Excited, he wrote Frederick in New York City and offered him a half interest in his venture. Frederick, who had kept abreast of all the California excitement, agreed that the land was a good buy and with his consent Jacob bought the property. The date of the sale was September 3, 1875. Frederick's part of the money arrived later and on December 11, 1875, half of the property was recorded in his name.

Jacob Beringer had by now reached the seasoned age of 31 and was anxious to start his new winery, while continuing to earn wages at Krug. Throughout the spring and summer of 1876 he tended his newly acquired vineyard, made his first crush, and that fall presumably with an infusion of capital from Frederick hired workmen to begin excavating for a new stone winery building against the hillside.

Plans had been drawn for a 44x103-foot two-story building to be constructed from local quarried stone. There would be a graded road cut into the hill behind the winery so wagons could unload grapes into a crusher on the flat roof, where the juice would flow by gravity into the fermenting tanks below. It was the classic European method the Beringers knew in Mainz, with grape processing on the upper floors and fermentation and aging on the lower floors. The horse teams took the loads to the highest point, and gravity did the rest. Although partly hidden by undergrowth, that old road behind the Beringer winery can still be seen along the hill today.

In his excavations for the building site, Jacob had made a fortunate discovery. The hillside beyond the foundation was almost solid limestone! It was perfect for excavating tunnels for barrel aging so he had his workmen build a stone archway facing the back wall on the ground floor of his new winery building. This would serve as the entrance to the new storeroom cave that he would have tunneled into the hill. St. Helena had its own small Chinatown and from here Beringer would recruit the laborers needed for the job. Furnished with blasting powder, picks and shovels, they would begin what would amount to many years of

tunneling, carrying the handworked limestone out to the waste heaps in baskets slung from shoulder boards.

The vineyard that came with the property consisted of about 28 acres planted to Riesling and Golden Chasselas. Jacob made his first wine from these grapes in 1876 while his winery was under construction. Ambitious, he also planted ornamental trees and lemons and oranges on the property, and graded the county road out front to spruce up the place. Water draining down Spring Mountain, that had been a problem, was diverted off the land into adjacent York Creek.

In the spring of 1878, Jacob Beringer was living the good bachelor life in the old "Hudson" house on the property. He had just left Charles Krug on amiable terms in February and was now working night and day supervising the construction of the new stone winery and the planting of additions to the vineyard. A part of the 1876 vintage had been sold off and 40,000 gallons of new wine was in process.

In the spring of 1879, Frederick's wife, Bertha, arrived from New York to visit her husband's St. Helena investment for the first time. It was also a good opportunity to meet her new sister-in-law, for Jacob, now a successful local businessman and member of the Town Board of Trustees, had married that April to Miss Agnes Tscheinig.

Bertha Beringer liked what she saw of the place and there was good reason. The winery was already bringing in revenue and over the coming years, it would continue to do so. In June 1879, Beringer Brothers shipped 14,000 gallons of wine from St. Helena, almost twice that of Charles Krug. The following spring Frederick, who was selling all the wine that his brother could ship, opened a store and wine cellar at 180 Fulton Street in New York City to handle Beringer as well as other fine wines.

Albert Schantzen, Beringer's bookkeeper in St. Helena, was sent east to manage the new enterprise. A shipment of 15,000 gallons of wine had already arrived in New York City and 20,000 gallons more were on their way. Thus Beringer Brothers were helping establish Napa Valley on the East Coast as a major source of premium table wines. And already some valley vintners were concerned about cheap imitators. An article in the December 19, 1879 *San Francisco Post* described the situation:

"In the St. Helena district some wines are made

Famed Mexican General Mariano Vallejo gave out the first Napa Valley land grants. David Hudson bought what is now the Beringer site after rising against him in the historic Bear Flag Revolt of 1846.

Charles Krug, one of the earliest Napa Valley winemakers, married Carolina Bale, grand-niece of Gen. Vallejo. Jacob Beringer worked for Krug before buying his own place next door in 1875.

The Beringer Land

Jacob and Frederick Beringer were the fourth titled owners of the St. Helena site purchased in 1875 to establish their winery.

Originally, this land was part of the huge Rancho Carne Humana land grant, one of many such "ranchos" offered by the Mexican government to help secure its claim to California after the revolt with Spain in 1821. The first tract given to a worthy settler in what is now Napa Valley went to George Yount, an American who had first arrived here in 1831. Yount's Mexican grant was equal to six square miles of land and extended from present-day Yountville to just beyond the small hamlet of Rutherford. The second tract was given to Dr. Edward Bale, and ran from Yount's grant to the present site of Calistoga.

DR. EDWARD BALE

Edward T. Bale was a physician who came to California in 1837. A hard-living adventurer, in 1839 he married Maria Ignacia Soberanes, a niece of General Mariano Vallejo. Soon afterwards, Bale found himself employed as a physician to Vallejo's Mexican garrison, then quartered in the Sonoma Pueblo. As payment for the doctor's loyalty and good services, Vallejo asked that Bale be given four square leagues of land in the adjoining valley, a request approved by Governor Juan Baptista Alvarado on June 23, 1841.

Bale established his hacienda south of the present city of St. Helena and shortly thereafter began building a grist mill on his land about five miles north. He also built a sawmill nearby and one of the first men employed there was David Hudson, who would soon assure himself a place in history as one of those who took part in the famed 1846 Bear Flag Revolt which helped win independence for California.

DAVID HUDSON

In the winter of 1845 David Hudson and his family arrived in California after crossing the plains from Missouri. Members of their party included John Grigsby and John York and they first settled in the Napa Valley near present Calistoga.

Later, when David Hudson went to work for Dr. Bale, he was one of the historic handful of men who plotted to wrest control of California away from Mexico. The result of their meetings took place one June morning in 1846 when Hudson, York, Grigsby and thirty-two other newly arrived American trappers and farmers rode into the undefended Pueblo of Sonoma, arrested General Vallejo, and declared California a Republic independent of Mexican rule. The banner they raised over Sonoma that day was their own creation and would become the official California state flag.

After the historic event, Hudson returned to his old job at the Bale mill. Then in 1848 he caught gold fever and joined Bale in the rush to the Sierras. Bale would die suddenly in 1849. Meanwhile, in December 1848, Hudson had panned enough to buy 300 acres of Bale's Napa Valley land for $10,000 in gold.

Hiring a neighbor named William Spurr to build him a fine two-story frame house on the property, Hudson, by now married, also planted a small vineyard and settled down to raise a family. Twenty-four years later he would sell the property to William Daegener for $25,000 in gold coin.

WILLIAM DAEGENER

Little is known about William Daegener except that he continued to improve on the property and vineyards. In September, 1875, two years after the purchase from Hudson, he sold the best 215 acres to Jacob and Frederick Beringer as the site for their now famous winery. ❧

C.J. DYER, DEL.

48

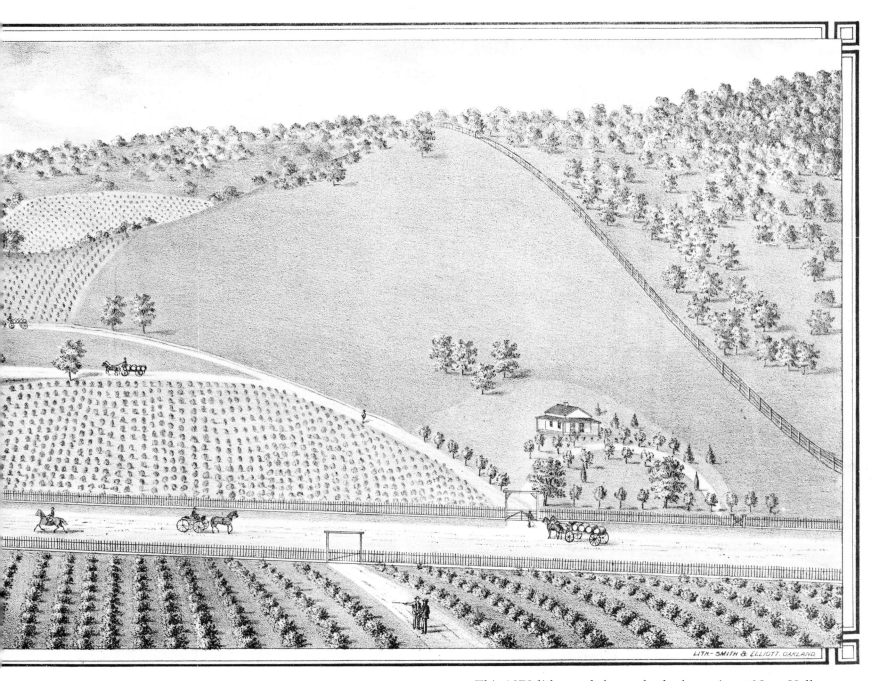

This 1879 lithograph from a book of prominent Napa Valley estates, depicts Beringer Brothers vineyards and winery before the stone cellar received its mansard-roofed third story, and before Frederick's Rhine House was built. It was erected in 1883 on the site of Jacob's old "Hudson house" residence (at the center of the opposite page), which was moved over in front of the cellar to make a more appropriate site for the mansion. Many of the trees and curved drives still remain but a low stone wall has replaced the picket fence out front. The public road (now Highway 29) has long since been planted to the "Tunnel of Elms."

Work started in 1876 on the Beringer wine cellar which was built against the hillside of native cut stone. At first it had a flat roof, or floor, used to unload grapes. Then in 1880 the third story and roof were added, topped by an observatory. Through an arch in the back wall Chinese workmen labored for years chiseling out the limestone tunnels used for barrel aging. Driven hundreds of feet into the mountain, the labyrinth of caves kept a perfect year-round temperature of 58 degrees and the black moss that grew on their walls proved a blessing, keeping the air dry and pure.

The winery with the new third-story in 1882. Barrel aging caves (below) were tunneled through its back wall.

Rare among Napa Valley wineries, the aging caves of Beringer were dug into the limestone hillside beginning in 1876 by Chinese labor.

Los Hermanos Vineyards.
BERINGER BROS.
Wine Growers and Distillers of Grape Brandy.
ST. HELENA,
NAPA COUNTY, CAL.

Grape brandy played an important role in the early success of Beringer Brothers. The distillery was in full operation by the mid-1880s, shipping carloads out of St. Helena to the East Coast and Europe. Heavily damaged by the 1906 earthquake, the stone building was rebuilt, shut down by Prohibition, reactivated, and finally torn down in the 1970s.

An 1890 display card.

Beringer's castle-like brandy distillery was built adjacent to their wine cellar in 1879.

simply because there is cheap temporary profit in them. These are the sweet wines, Port, Sherry, a dreadful article called 'mountain wine' and others that shall be nameless . . . all of these are wines more or less fabricated and can be made anywhere. As the traffic in the real wines increase that business will undoubtedly locate itself away from the vineyards . . ."

Competition was becoming keen and to meet it Jacob continued construction on the winery complex, including a smaller one-story brandy building south of the main cellar. The mason work was done by Henry Malone, whose stone artistry drew praise from locals. The *St. Helena Star* reported that the new distillery building was finished with "an extra fine front," while others described the facade as "castle-like."

In late 1879, the ornate distillery building was completed, just in time for the installation of a huge four-ton steam boiler and some other brandy-making equipment which Jacob had bought from a defunct distillery in Sonoma. Jacob solved the difficult problem of getting it to St. Helena by dismantling the heavy piece and hauling it around the steep mountains through Napa in two wagon loads. The 3x14-foot boiler, which would be used to provide steam for distillation, was set at the north end of the building.

Inside the winery, Chinese workers by now had driven 45 feet into the mountain. The tunnel's 17-foot width allowed for a row of casks on each side with a six-foot passageway between them. It was an ideal arrangement for the aging of the best wines, with room for moving the barrels back and forth in the tunnel.

By the end of 1879 the limestone caves were sunk into the mountain 70 feet when Jacob made the decision to "drift" from the main tunnel, cutting chambers on both sides. He calculated that it was cheaper to tunnel for cellar space than construct more outside buildings. It was a decision that would forever establish the unique character of his winery, as compared to others in the Napa Valley.

In early 1880 the Beringers bought another 70 acres of mountain land at the 1,000 foot level behind the winery. That spring they cleared and planted sixteen of these acres in more vines, contributing something to the growing acreage throughout the state. By the end of the year there were more than 150,000 acres under vine in California as serious vintners and speculators alike discovered its near perfect growing conditions.

By 1886 the handsome Beringer cellar was one of the most-prestigious wine producers in the Napa Valley, shipping worldwide.

Pictured today, details of a window shows the artistry of the winery's original stone masons.

The brothers located their winery building against the hillside to take advantage of gravity flow, as was the custom in their native Rhine Valley. The picket fence marks the upper road where wagon loads of grapes were brought to the crusher, then the juice was sluiced down to the lower floors. Jacob kept an efficient operation. At the right he is pictured with a new device used to cork bottles.

Jacob Beringer on the ground level of his cellar.

At the Beringer winery, the big steam boiler had been set up as a stationary engine rigged with a system of belts and pulleys to do a variety of chores besides distilling brandy. Its wood-fired power was not only harnessed to the grape crusher but was running the feed-grinding mill for the horses and the saw for cutting fire wood. Its belts also ran a lift-conveyor that moved the grapes from the wagons to the chute over the crushing unit.

Jacob's plan was to crush about 80 tons of grapes per day, an enormous task by hand. With the use of steam power he was able to mount his crusher on top of a tank car on tracks. The men could then roll the juice to the different roof hatches and dump it into the fermenting tanks below at a big savings in labor.

Jacob was not only ingenious but prudent. As the dollars rolled in, he reinvested them in more vineyards, space and equipment. In late 1880 the third story and sloped roof of the main building were added, with the former asbestos-topped flat roof of the building now the floor of the third story. Thirty-two new thousand-gallon redwood casks were installed and a footbridge was built to connect the second floor of the main cellar with the roof of the fermenting cellar.

"They have also built on top of all a neat observatory, not unlike the pilot house of a steamer," reported the *St. Helena Star*, "large enough for several persons to sit in at once, where a most delightful view is had of all the valley from Yountville to Lodi (district)."

The brothers' activity continued to be big news in St. Helena as recorded in this glowing item from the *Star* in the October 27, 1882, edition: "Beringer Brothers at their beautiful place on York Creek are always the admiration of the visitor and a model of neat and tasteful arrangement. Their handsome buildings present an inspiring appearance to the passerby and their steam machinery—is a model of rapid work."

In March 1883, an "artificial stone" floor was laid in the main winery cellar and vaults to cover the dirt floor. It consisted of poured concrete blocks two-feet square and three-inches thick cast in place, and designed for rough use, so that "even the riveted metal hoops on the heavy casks would not mar the surface." Curbing was also installed to keep water from standing beneath the casks.

Due to the great distance between New York City and the West Coast by train, Frederick Beringer did not

Master winemaker Jacob Beringer poses in front of his winery with his daughter Bertha and two workers in 1886. The man at the right is a cooper making final adjustments to barrels of wine ready for shipment. In the distance is Howell Mountain and beyond Jacob's right shoulder is Charles Krug winery where he worked when first arriving in California. The east-west boundary between the two properties ran through the adjoining vineyards, across the railroad tracks and down to the Napa River.

often visit his property in St. Helena. But when he did, it was occasion to throw a party. On one such visit in May 1883, Frederick and Jacob hosted a wine tasting at the winery home and private cellars.

A heavy downpour prevented their Sonoma guests from making the long trip across the mountains, but other eminent vintners from the upper Napa Valley such as William Scheffler, Charles Krug, John Thomann and W.W. Lyman did attend. Just before his trip to California, Frederick had been in Europe and brought back many fine wines, some of which he brought with him on the trip to Napa Valley. After lunch, some of the local winemakers' best vintages were tasted and to the men's delight, scored favorably against the European samples.

Life in the pleasant Napa Valley moved along at an easy pace, a fact that made Frederick envious. For years he had been the ambitious city businessman piling up his wealth, but now it was clear to him that Jacob had the real life. It was the simple pleasures of coming back to the house after a long day's work at the winery, to a home-grown dinner and perhaps old cronies over for a glass of wine on the porch.

Before returning to New York City, Frederick made his decision, announcing that he and his family intended to make their home in the Napa Valley. The news was duly reported in the florid journalistic style of the time in the May 13, 1883, *St. Helena Star:*

"Indeed he (Frederick Beringer) exhibited to friends plans of a fine large dwelling in the Gothic style which it was intended to erect on the site of the present one, and which we hope soon to see built not only as a still further ornament to their beautiful premises but as a fitting home for the friends whose enterprise and public spirit we are all so much indebted."

Exactly what the arrangement was is lost to history but Frederick had Jacob move his house out of the way so he could start the foundation of his own home. It is assumed that Frederick had put in the most capital and was now being rewarded with the best homesite. In any event, work was begun that same year on the stone foundation of his home close to York Creek. At the same time, the Beringer's erected a large new horse barn on their property across Main Street. It was finished by August and a gala barn warming was announced.

Colorful Chinese lanterns illuminated the barn

during the event as friends from Calistoga, Rutherford, Oakville and Yountville danced from night till dawn. During breaks in the dancing and festivities, Jacob extended an open invitation to everyone for a glass of Napa Valley wine in his private cellar. It was the beginning of a Beringer tradition.

Over the next two years, more new buildings were added to the Beringer estate. In 1885, stables, a carriage house and a boarding house for employees were built across the street from Frederick's new mansion, which was now the talk of the valley. Excavation of the winery caves continued as workers reached a full 100 feet into the mountain.

By 1886 Beringer Brothers was producing about 175,000 gallons of wine using steam-driven equipment described in awe by the *St. Helena Star* as "near perfect in its line as things earthly can be." The major competition, Charles Krug, was making about 225,000 gallons of wine per year.

The crush of 1889 was a disaster for the Napa Valley. A cool summer had lowered grape sugars, while the dread phylloxera ravaged the vines. "The phylloxera is marching at such a rate," reported the October 11, 1889, *Star*, "that if not checked will destroy some vineyards in two years. If nothing is done there will be practically no vineyards left in Napa Valley. As for the remedy, there is only one so far known to man and that is to plant resistants. If we wish to guard this grand industry from annihilation the resistant vine will be our only preservation."

Phylloxera is a destructive little plant louse that somehow found its way from the eastern United States to France in the 1860s. Over the next twenty years, it devastated nearly all of the vineyards of Bordeaux, Burgundy and Champagne, as well as most other vineyards of Europe and California. North American grapes, however, were resistant to phylloxera, so the solution for eliminating the louse from the world's vineyards was to graft onto native North American roots. It was a bitter piece of irony that saw the source

Jacob ran the winery, while Frederick provided the money. In work shoes and vest the industrious vintner is pictured with his wealthy brother and their workers in front of the cellar in 1895. Between them is six year-old Charles, Jacob's youngest son, who would one day be winery president. A cellarman's day was long, the pay was low, and shirt sleeves stained to the elbows with grape juice marked his trade.

Jacob and his family lived in the "old Hudson house," one of the earliest homes in the valley, which came with the property when the brothers bought it in 1875. Situated below the winery, it was remodeled and expanded to accommodate his growing family and many visiting guests. At the right some Beringer family members and friends gather on the ample front steps of the home in 1890. Left to right are Mrs. Jacob Schram, wife of the eminent Calistoga vintner; (unidentified); Jacob; Frederick's wife Bertha; Jacob's wife Agnes (holding daughter Agnes); Martha; Bertha; Eda (Frederick's daughter); and young Otto Beringer.

Jacob's two-story home, left, built by the pioneer David Hudson c. 1850, with the distillery and winery buildings beyond.

Family and friends gathered on Jacob's popular front porch.

The Beringer brothers were proud of their wines and entered them in contests throughout the U.S. and abroad. Publicity from the many ribbons and medals won was a prime reason for their early marketing success. At the left (obverse and reverse) is the Gold Medal awarded Beringer Zinfandel at the 1915 San Francisco fair.

The 1915 Panama-Pacific International Exposition held in San Francisco.

Jacob Beringer, left, and Jacob Schram.

At the turn-of-the-century the upper Napa Valley was humored by the "three Jakes," Jacob Beringer, Jacob Schram, and Jacob Grimm. All were German winemakers and lasting friends whose happy singing on their frequent buggy rides was legendary. Schram (Schramsberg) and Grimm had wineries in Calistoga and the former is pictured (in beard) visiting Jacob Beringer with two friends sbout 1904.

of the problem eventually become part of the solution.

While the deadly phylloxera battle was being waged and won in the vineyards, Beringer wines in 1889 were gaining worldwide recognition. That year they won a coveted Silver Medal for their Riesling entry at the Paris Exposition, an award that sparked a boom of foreign orders. A half carload of wine was shipped to Tokyo, and another to Berlin, and later that summer they sent 800 barrels of their acclaimed brandy via the British ship *Dunfillan* to Liverpool.

At their handsome stone winery, meanwhile, plans were being carried out to take advantage of the increased business. The labyrinth of aging tunnels bored into the limestone had now reached a combined length of 450 feet, and a series of new 500 gallon upright oak aging casks had been installed in the front cellars with the latest hydraulic transfer pumps. By the end of the 1889 crush there were 230,000 gallons stored in the winery, including 80,000 gallons from 1888.

Fame and good fortune were smiling on the two likeable German brothers and in the years following the great phylloxera epidemic leading up to the turn-of-the-century, Los Hermanos was their Garden of Eden. They enjoyed planting their grounds with exotic botanical specimens, and playing hosts to the many friends and distinguished visitors who arrived by carriage on their fine curved drives. A visit almost always included a tour of the cool private cellars of the two adjacent homes to sample some of the best vintages. After lunch with close friends meant wine talk, political gossip, or perhaps a game of whist on the veranda, or dozing in the shade. And between the two brothers, there were now nine Beringer children on the premises to make life interesting. Frederick and his wife had Frederick, Jr., Eda, and Anita. Jacob and Agnes had Jacob, Jr., Charles, Otto, Bertha, Martha, and Agnes. Days were filled with frolic and laughter as the two families grew up together.

Frederick Beringer reigned over Rhine House like a generous old baron and was adored by his family. He entertained royally and was considered one of the community's leading citizens, having established the Savings Bank of St. Helena, a creamery, and assisted with the financing of the new high school. As for the big city life he was accustomed to, he had made friends in San Francisco and often spent time there enjoying the social scene with his family. Thus it came as a great

Looking northwest through Jacob's elms about 1905.

A cut stone wall replaced the picket fence in front of Beringer winery by the turn-of-the-century. A driver is pictured with his team at the main entrance. Sometime during this period Jacob planted the county road out front with the trees that would become St. Helena's famous "Tunnel of Elms."

St. Helena's buggy-lined Main Street in 1898. Many of the town's fine old store fronts are familiar landmarks today.

St. Helena, California

THE home of Beringer winery is St. Helena, one of the most picturesque towns in California. "I wish I could describe it in a way to suggest its real charm and beauty," wrote one impressed visitor in 1909. "It would mean hard times for Southern California. Everybody endowed with an auto would be headed here."

Historically, the town's roots go back to 1853 when Henry Still, an English immigrant, bought one hundred acres of the Carne Humana Rancho Mexican land grant from Maria Bale, widow of the grantee Dr. Edward T. Bale. Still's land lay west of the dirt trail which is now Main Street, between Sulphur Creek and what is now Madrona Avenue, and it was along this lightly travelled frontage that he erected a split-redwood shanty and opened a general store. The place was about eight miles either way to the settlements of Calistoga and Yountville and he surmised correctly that the time would come for a bustling town here in the heart of what was becoming a rich farming section.

To hedge his bet, Still was soon giving away free lots to anyone who would put up a business building and by 1855 neighboring new store fronts included John Kister's harness shop and a small hotel erected by A. Tainter. Christian Turkeldson erected another store in 1856, which was followed by the opening of a blacksmith shop, a wagon and carriage maker, and a small mercantile store opened by W.A. Elgin. As the town took shape, other entrepreneurs began developing the other side of the road, and laying out streets. One of the first residences was erected by H. Dickson and soon others were established.

One legend has it that Still named his infant town after "St. Helena," a chapter of the Sons of Temperance established here about 1856. A more logical theory is that he simply named it for Mount St. Helena, whose high peak majestically fills the horizon about a dozen miles distant, beyond Calistoga.

The railroad arrived in 1868, putting St. Helena on the map and connecting it to other towns in the Napa Valley, as well as to commerce in San Francisco via the Bay ferries from Vallejo. On March 4, 1876, the town was incorporated and by now it was the hub of a flourishing wine industry, as well as terminus for the outlying hamlet of Pope Valley, and for vacationers visiting some of the local hot springs resorts.

By 1881 the population of St. Helena had reached 1,400 and its business section, which stretched for about a half mile along Main Street, included nine stores, six saloons, and five hotels. It also had five blacksmith's shops, three livery stables, a hardware store, two wagon shops, three barber shops, two drug stores, two lumber yards, one newspaper, one bakery, one tailor and a telegraph office.

Tracks were laid down Main Street for a new interurban electric train that went into service on New Year's Day, 1908. But despite the easier access to bigger population centers, St. Helena somehow avoided a building boom and from 1905 to 1975 barely doubled its population to about 4,000. Still retaining much of the charm of its earlier years, it is home today to some of America's most famous wineries including Beringer, Charles Krug, Christian Brothers, Louis Martini and Sutter Home. ❧

Main Street looking northwest from Gibbs Stables near Sulphur Creek in the 1890's.

St. Helenans W.A. Bingham and J.W. Castner talking politics on Main Street in 1902.

Busy hub of the Napa Valley wine trade, St. Helena's streets saw many interesting characters in its early boom, including popular writers Ambrose Bierce and Robert Louis Stevenson. Pictured above about 1905, prominent local wine men Frank Pellet, left, and Bismark Bruck trade observations. Bruck had succeeded his late uncle Charles Krug in the operation of his winery.

Jacob Beringer, right, with friends and his hallmark carved cask mounted for the winery's entry in St. Helena's 1911 Vintage Festival parade. The 2700-gallon cask with its double "B" monogram was probably carved by Mssr. Schaer, a noted San Francisco craftsman who went to work for the winery in 1879. In later years the cask served as a photo backdrop for celebrities visiting the winery.

shock to everyone when, in 1899, at the very prime of his life, Frederick was diagnosed with Bright's disease. Despite all efforts to save him his condition steadily grew worse until the end came on July 12, 1901, when he died at his St. Helena home.

Frederick "Fritz" Beringer's casket was on view all day of the funeral in the Rhine House parlor as hundreds of friends and colleagues arrived to pay their respects. Charles Bundschu, a prominent San Francisco wine merchant, delivered the eulogy and more than a hundred carriages were in the solemn procession to the cemetery up Spring Street.

But life went on at Los Hermanos. Then, five years later another shock hit the winery. In April 1906, Jacob was in San Francisco that fateful day when the great earthquake struck. When he managed to return home the next morning, he discovered that the town and his winery had suffered extensive damage. The front and back walls of the ornate brandy distillery had crumbled under the jolt and the stone winery building was also badly damaged.

In Napa, 18 miles south of St. Helena, nearly all of the chimneys were knocked down. Many of the San Francisco homeless were sent to Napa by ferry boat where they were sheltered at the city park and St. Helena volunteers sent them a wagon load of bread and cooked food to help out.

For the next few years, Jacob continued to promote his wines and winery, while rebuilding from the earthquake. Then, in April 1909, he took a tour abroad to visit his old home town in Germany—a place he hadn't seen in forty years. Accompanying him by train as far as New York were his daughters Bertha and Martha, who would visit with relatives until their father's return in August. The trip to Mainz was filled with nostalgia and when he arrived home he had a fresh new outlook on life. From now on he would shift more of the responsibility for running the business to his adult children, while he began to enjoy more of the quiet life of his home and gardens.

By now the Beringer vineyards amounted to about 120 acres, producing 400 tons of grapes annually. It was enough that the winery didn't have to buy grapes from other growers and plenty, along with cellar work, to keep the three Beringer sons in the business. Boys "Jake" and Otto married (Jake to Adela Rammers in 1912, and Otto to Ethel Baxter in 1913) and continued

Young Beringers and friends clown in front of the winery in 1904. Jacob's daughters Martha (top, center) and Bertha (top, right) enjoyed an active social life but never married. They would live out their lives as spinsters in the family's old "Hudson house" on the property where they were born.

to work for their father. Young Charles also worked at the winery but seemed more interested in getting an education and striking out on his own.

In 1911 the City of St. Helena inaugurated its first Vintage Festival celebration to coincide with the fall crush. Beringer Brothers' parade entry would be a huge oak cask with their initials "BB" carved in the end that would later go on display along with other exhibits in the exposition tent. It was good local publicity and in succeeding years Jacob Beringer made sure they were well represented. The 1914 tent exhibit consisted of a reproduction of the distillery building in bottle corks and in 1915 was an open-ended barrel lined with cream of tartar to show prohibitionists an essential by-product of the grape. Ample displays of the firm's wines in bottles and barrels showed the full line of Zinfandels, Burgundies, Cabernets, Sauternes, Rieslings, and Brandies.

A major event for 1915 was the Panama-Pacific International Exposition held in San Francisco. Naturally the Beringer family attended and walked away with many awards in the wine judging, including Gold Medals for their Grape Brandy and for their Zinfandel and Burgundy entries.

The late Frederick Beringer's widow, Bertha, and her offspring had some time before moved to San Francisco. They were no longer interested in the winery and in 1914 asked amicably to have Beringer Brothers incorporated so Jacob's side of the family could buy them out of their shares. That same year Bertha sold her beloved Rhine House mansion and its grounds to a wealthy Fresno couple for use as a summer home. And so it was that one of St. Helena's most glamorous chapters had come to a close.

Los Hermanos was crumbling. The world was at war, and on October 23, 1915, after two years of failing health, the remaining founder Jacob Beringer would pass away at his home in St. Helena at the age of 71. It was truly the end of an era, for with Jacob went all the driving force behind the winery. Left to run it were his widow Agnes, and any of his six grown children who would step into his shoes. That moment would come before the end of the year when the youngest son, Charles, was made president of Beringer Brothers and his sister Bertha was named secretary-manager.

These were difficult times, made all the worse by ominous talk of national prohibition. ❧

Jacob Beringer's well-kept home (Hudson house) about the time of his death in 1915.

Retired from the rigors of winery business, Jacob Beringer poses with his wife Agnes and their offspring on the steps of his home in 1914. The children, left to right, are: Otto, Agnes, Charles, Martha, Bertha and Jacob. Following the pioneer Napa Valley vintner's death in 1915, his son Charles and daughter Bertha would run the winery. The late Frederick's family had sold to Jacob's. In the end, Otto's two children held control.

The Rhine House

Frederick's Mansion

SET against the hillside and spreading oaks of the Beringer estate is the Rhine House, the most elegant home of all the old Napa Valley wine families.

Built in 1883-84, it is a classic example of that grand American period we have since labeled "the Victorian Age," a time when ponderously over-decorated mansions were considered the ultimate show of wealth.

Prosperous wine broker Frederick Beringer had envied the great mansions of New York City and had been a part of high society while in business there. He wanted to build a monument to his own success and when he invested with his brother in the Napa Valley, he decided to build it here in St. Helena where it would have little competition. His new California villa would be reminiscent of the family's impressive old German home at Mainz-on-the-Rhine where the Beringer brothers grew up.

In early 1883, when he announced plans to begin building his residence, there was already a house on the Beringer property. This was Jacob's two story "old Hudson house" that dated back to about 1850 and came with the place when the brothers purchased it. The farmhouse stood in the perfect setting for a mansion so Frederick, as principal supplier of capital in the partnership, simply asked his brother to move his home over about two hundred feet to make room for a structure more worthy of the site.

Jacob obliged. Moving a house was no difficult feat in those days with no plumbing or electricity to disconnect. It was common practice to raise them and roll them to a new location on a rotation of heavy logs.

The foundation cornerstone-laying ceremony for the new winery mansion would take place in September, 1883, while Frederick and his wife were at their home in New York. Jacob played host to the large gathering while one of his brother's close San Francisco friends, Dr. J.A. Bauer, delivered the dedication.

Afterwards the guests in attendance enjoyed several glasses of California champagne. Then, a bottle full was poured ceremoniously on the cornerstone. Various coins, photographs of the Beringer family, clippings from San Francisco and Napa journals, cards of attending guests and samples of wines made on the place were then placed in large glass jars to be sealed up in the stone. With these was a telegram just arrived from Frederick Beringer; "Let the new building be the home of peace, brotherly love and good fellowship with all."

" . . . The laying of a cornerstone," wrote the editor of the *St. Helena Star*, "where only a few dozen years ago the grizzly bear and the Indian warrior fought and quarrelled about the wild fruits on this very ground, where now the Johannisberg, the Zinfandel and the Riesling grow to the delight of all sensible and jolly people, who comprehend that the noble and generous wine is necessary to the happiness of the human race."

"Rhine House" was two years in the building and of course the columns of the local paper were richly padded with journalistic description concerning the construction and embellishment of what was rapidly becoming St. Helena's pride. From the cupola atop its eighty foot tower to the vast wine cellar which occupied the entire basement, not a single detail was overlooked, right down to the last tasseled portiere.

"The building is in the medieval style" choralled the *Star*. "Basement and first story are of locally quarried limestone. The second story is of bricks sheathed in California redwood. Above this is a begabled attic replete with many dormer windows along with a tower which is higher than any steeple in town. The building, aside from a few artistic irregularities is nearly seventy feet square and with the addition of the large conservatory, presents a facade 120 feet long. With its stone and brick construction crowned with a roof of slates imported from Pennsylvania, the house may be regarded as almost completely immune from fire.

"On the rear of the main building is a large wing, on the lower floor of which is the kitchen, laundry, pantries, butler's room, etc. On the upper floor the servants apartments are located." No mention was made of the fact that the house contained an independent gas plant for lighting, and indoor plumbing, which in the mid-eighties were novelties enjoyed by the well-to-do.

The ornate stained glass panels used in the doors and overwindows, were personally created for Frederick Beringer at a cost of more than $6,000. (In this day a very comfortable home could have been built for considerably less). Jewelled art glass was all the rage in the 1880s and certainly no self-respecting mansion on the West Coast was without at least one such window in the parlor and another grander one on the stair landing. Tiffany & Company of New York became a major supplier, but they were only one of a dozen such eastern firms to fabricate these colorful adornments. Those in the Beringer house were done by a New York artist named Lambert.

"Hunting scenes are portrayed on the grand staircase while William Shakespeare keeps watch from a window in the library. Wild flowers and butterflies adorn the upper windows of the parlor while the dining room panes portray trout, game and still life to stimulate the palate." So wrote the *St. Helena Star*. "Visitors to the home are greeted by two Shakespearian knights portrayed in the large stained glass panels set in the pair of front doors. These two figures are said to be Jacob and Frederick Beringer."

The foundation, wine cellar, and facade of Frederick Beringer's impressive "Rhine House" mansion were built of hand-cut stone from a local quarry. Here, in September, 1883, following dedication ceremonies as friends and contractors look on, a workman seals the inscribed cornerstone. At the right is Jacob Beringer who supervised the work while his brother was in the East.

Built at a cost of about $30,000, Rhine House is pictured a few years after its completion in 1884. A classic example of Victorian architecture with its many gables, turrets and ornaments, the seventeen-room mansion would be home to Frederick Beringer and his family until shortly after the turn-of-the-century. This view shows the glass-enclosed conservatory off the south portico where Frederick tended botanical specimens.

An elegant gable ornamenting the mansion's 80-foot tower is typical of the intricate woodwork throughout. Except for 1906 earthquake repairs, the original roof of Pennsylvania slate is just as it was laid in 1883.

For a baronial mansion, the lavish use of wood marquetry and parquetry was the expected thing. True to its kind, the floors of the house were carpeted in the finest French moque with the borders in every room of oak inlaid with mahogany, satinwood, maple and walnut.

The gentleman who orchestrated all this was the talented architect Albert Schroepfer of San Francisco. Schroepfer also designed other fine residences in Napa Valley including Miravalle, the palatial home of Tiburcio Parrott which has since gained renown as the setting for the TV drama, *Falcon Crest*. Parrott, scion of one of San Francisco's most prestigious families, was a close friend of the Beringers and his estate was located directly behind theirs on Spring Mountain Road.

Contractors for the Rhine House were locals Joseph Cudlon and Charles Martini. Mariano Bale, son of the pioneer Dr. Bale, supervised the carpentry.

By 1884 the Rhine House was ready for occupancy by the Beringers. Today, one may only imagine what went on in that "best of all possible worlds." With the six great bedrooms filled with family and members of San Francisco's elite, there were certainly the usual rounds of dinners, teas, picnics and balls. Someone has aptly described country life in such houses of that period as one of "vigorous inactivity". Certainly Jacob's family, living in the comfortable old "Hudson" house just a stone's throw away, enjoyed more than a nibble of the rich life next door.

Entering Rhine House by way of the broad double doors off the front portico, the 1880s visitor found himself in a large reception hall 24x36 feet in size. To the right was the large parlor finished in cedar. It was separated by folding doors and hung with elegant curtains looped on either side. To the left of the hall was Frederick's library and the dining room. The cozy library was lined with bookcases and ornamented with statuary and paintings—the perfect setting for a quiet afternoon's reading. Off this opened a small smoking room where gentlemen could spend a pleasant half-hour after dinner with their brandy and cigars.

From the spacious dining room, company could stroll across the veranda to the glass enclosed conservatory which afforded an excellent view of the gardens with its sloping lawns shaded by massive oaks and colored by many-hued flowers.

Overnight guests were shown their rooms up the

A Rhine House window by Lambert depicting waterfowl.

One of the many jeweled art glass windows complementing the fine stonework of Frederick Beringer's mansion.

The two brothers from Germany did well in the California wine business. Frederick Beringer and his wife pose for a portrait with Jacob, right, and his wife on the veranda of Frederick's imposing St. Helena mansion in 1891. The youngsters are Jacob's son Otto and daughter Bertha, two of the nine children between the families.

beautiful staircase off the reception hall to the second floor. Here, in addition to the three family bedrooms, were three guest chambers "large and fitted up with all the modern improvements, each so admirably arranged as to be well lighted, airy and cheerful." Another stairway led to the garret (third) floor which was left unfinished but could easily be made into three or four more bedrooms.

Throughout the mansion large Turkish rugs complimented the beautifully polished hardwood floors and every room was elegantly furnished and set off with handsome paintings and works of fine art.

The house was a masterpiece of Victorian architecture and Frederick Beringer and his family enjoyed its splendor for eighteen wonderful years. Then, in 1901, tragedy struck. After a lingering illness, Frederick passed to his reward from the great upstairs bedroom which is today known as the "Founder's Room." With his death the great days at the Rhine House had come to an end. For his widow, Bertha Beringer, now preferred to live out her sorrow in the more active surroundings that the social life in San Francisco had to offer. She would move there to be nearer her grown children and the big house would remain empty except when the family vacationed there in the summer.

Rhine House would mainly gather cobwebs for the next decade. In 1906 the local paper, inventorying the damage caused by the earthquake in the Napa Valley, did mention the house and its huge chimney that had crashed through the slate roof, and that some of the fine windows were damaged. That these items were repaired and the grounds generally kept up in good condition may be assumed, however, by another article in the *St. Helena Star*. This time by a 1909 item submitted by Horatio Stoll, secretary of the Grape Growers of California on his impressions of the valley; " . . . As you pass the Beringer villa near St. Helena, you cannot but be impressed with the air of refinement and prosperity that is evidenced everywhere. There are many handsome homes, with extensive park-like grounds, all kept in perfect condition."

Stoll also commented on the transportation of the day, "The roads are excellent and automobiles are to be seen everywhere. In fact, I doubt if there is any community of equal size that can boast of more. We also encountered many smart traps, filled with summery girls, and one of our best-known San Francisco bankers

riding a spirited black animal that fairly glistened in the morning sunshine."

Standing empty most of the time, Rhine House was a sad monument to another time. The Victorian era was over and with its demise went the ideas of family dynasties and of great houses that would impress for generations.

When the opportunity came, the widow Beringer sold the great old mansion and its adjoining grounds to Mr. and Mrs. Charles Teague, wealthy young citrus growers from Fresno. The Teagues would make some improvements such as electricity and modern plumbing, then rename their handsome estate "Trevor Terrace." It would be their summer residence, with the rest of their time divided between the ranch in Fresno and a suite at the Palace Hotel in San Francisco.

The Teagues made quite a social splash in St. Helena and entertained lavishly when they were in town. But thirteen years later their fortune ran out and the story of Rhine House would take another twist. It was 1927 and four years before the Teagues had used the house to secure a $5,000 promissory note to Mrs. Beringer. Bertha later sold the note to Dr. and Mrs. Myron Booth of St. Helena. The Teagues defaulted on the loan so the Rhine House was seized and sold at public auction to pay $400 unpaid interest on the note. At the auction Dr. Booth tendered the highest bid, picking up the mansion, all of its furnishings, the unpaid note and interest, for approximately the cost of the original stained glass windows—$6,000 cash!

Dr. Booth, a friend of the Charles Krug family across from Beringer, had long admired Rhine House, even before he moved his practice from San Francisco to St. Helena in 1921. In his hands the mansion would now get the care and dignity it deserved as the highly regarded country doctor brought up his own family in its elegant surroundings. And it wasn't long before the house again had a Beringer family connection, for one of Booth's daughters would marry Arthur Beringer, son of the winery president Charles Beringer.

The Booths owned the house for nineteen years. Then, in late 1945 the doctor and his wife sold it to Beringer Brother, Inc., for a reported $10,000 in a transaction orchestrated by winery manager Fred Abruzzini. According to the *Star*, "The house and its nearly three acres of gardens is thus restored to the winery property, and will be used, not for residence, but in

The symbol of the Arion Society, Frederick's longtime affiliation in New York City, adorns a bedroom gable.

A chimney falling through the slate roof was the most damage to Rhine House during the 1906 earthquake which badly jolted St. Helena. During this time Frederick's widow used the ornate mansion as a summer home, living most of the time in San Francisco which was devastated by the great quake.

Exquisite details of the front tower.

Rhine House as it appeared about 1913 with its original color scheme, awnings, and ornamental gardens.

connection with the operation of the plant . . . Sentimental reasons prompted the purchase by Beringer Bros., it is reported."

World War II had just ended and it was the Beringer intention to use the famous old mansion as a hospitality house for the expected hordes of post-war visitors with lots of new leisure time. But money, tires and gasoline were still scarce, as were the visitors, so the Rhine House sat empty again.

Two years later, in 1948, Beringer winery received a contract from United Airlines to furnish wine for in-flight service, which opened another brief chapter in the saga of Rhine House. One of the company officers negotiating the deal fell so in love with the gothic structure that he made a side offer, which was duly recorded in that week's issue of the local paper. "A new guest house will open in St. Helena shortly," reported the *Star*, "with the announcement that Beringer Bros. have leased the big stone house until recently owned by Dr. M.M. Booth and earlier the old Beringer home, to Edward Smith, secretary of United Airlines. Smith will convert the house into an exclusive hostel, catering to a selected clientele."

Smith renamed Frederick Beringer's old mansion the "Manor House" and operated it for about a year as a country inn with rooms and a restaurant before it folded for lack of business. It was something of a "bed and breakfast" idea that was just a few decades ahead of its time. There were plenty of people visiting the valley's world famous wineries by now, but few who came to spend the weekend.

Once again, Rhine House sat vacant. Until a few years later when C. Francis Reisner came on the scene. He was a former boxer, song writer and movie director with a heart condition, looking for a quiet job in the country. Winery manager Fred Abruzzini offered him a room upstairs in the big house if he would take charge of hospitality. Reisner accepted and for the next decade would reside at the mansion as Beringer's official "glad-hander," entertaining visitors with his gallery of movie lore until the guides came to take them on tours.

Wine World acquired the winery in 1971 and expanded on the role of the Rhine House as a center of hospitality. Since then it has been visited by thousands of winery guests annually, little changed from the grand days when Fredrick entertained there. ❧

A carved oak staircase leads to the upper bedrooms past jeweled windows with wild flowers and hunting scenes. Opposite: the double doors of the front entry have stained glass panels portraying Shakespearean knights. Legend says the two knights are actually Frederick and Jacob Beringer. Today the large entry room with its magnificent German white oak wainscoat and inlaid floors is used after visitor hours for special dinners.

The Rhine House during one of St. Helena's rare snowfalls.

Surviving Prohibition

Bertha Beringer

*T*HE seeds of total prohibition in the United States were sewn long before the Volstead Act of 1919 outlawed alcoholic beverages.

As early as 1900, prohibitionists were gaining ground against the "evils of drink," successively creating dry counties and putting pressure on anyone engaged in the liquor business. As the debate between the "Drys" and the "Wets" raged among the nation's lawmakers and in its newspapers, Napa Valley winemakers were becoming increasingly alarmed. "Combined with a successful agitation against the open saloon," wrote the editor of the *St. Helena Star* in a May, 1909, column, "good, well-meaning, but misguided people have suddenly determined that the viticultural industry is all wrong and must go with the rest. In their zeal the agitators would prohibit the

manufacture and sale of wine, have the grape vine pulled up by the roots and the great cellars left empty."

It is a matter of history that the "Drys" won. By 1914, when the First World War broke out in Europe, thirty-three states had already gone dry, and six years later the movement would claim the entire nation.

Against this scenario, at the beginning of 1916, Charles and Bertha Beringer found themselves the youthful managers of one of California's most distinguished wineries. Charles, at 27, was president of the firm, now owned wholly by his mother Agnes (Jacob's widow) Beringer and her children. Bertha, 32, ran the Beringer Brothers winery as secretary-manager. Taking less demanding responsibilities would be Jacob, Jr. "Jake" as winery foreman, Otto as cellarman, and Martha in the bottling department. Their sister, Agnes

While other cellars failed, quiet but tenacious Bertha Beringer managed her winery through the industry's greatest crisis.

Bertha Beringer supervises work in the aging tunnels.

Bertha Beringer in her mid-twenties.

A survivor, Beringer Sherry bottled after Repeal from stock illegal to sell during Prohibition carries the vintage date 1922.

RED WINES	Per Gal.
Claret .... $	.30
Claret, Sup.	.35
Claret, Extra Old	.43
Zinfandel	.40
Zinfandel, Sup.	.50
Zinfandel, Exta Old	.63
Burgundy	.43
Burgundy, Sup.	.58
Carignan	.65
Cabernet	.85

WHITE WINES	Per Gal.
Hock .... $	.38
Hock, Sup.	.47
Riesling	.50
Riesling, Sup.	.60
Riesling, Extra Old	.75
Sauterne	.80
Gutedel	.90
Mosel	.65
Mosel, Sup.	.85

Different varieties of grapes for making high class wines are grown special in our own vineyards.

SWEET WINES	Per Gal.
Sherry, A1. .... $	.70
Sherry, O.P.S.	.80
Port, A1.	.65
Port, O.P.S.	.75
Angelica, A1.	.70
Angelica, O.P.S.	.80
Muscatel, A1.	.70
Muscatel, O.P.S.	.80
Tokay, A1.	.80
Tokay, O.P.S.	.90

CALIFORNIA BRANDIES	Per Gal.
1908 .... $	2.85
1909	2.50
New	2.25

All brandies are made by Beringer Bros., Inc., and aged in the Bonded Warehouse at St. Helena.

Pure Altar Wines Our Specialty

This 1914 price list indicates what Beringer had to sell before Prohibition. For thirteen years (1920-33) wine and other such beverages could not be sold to the public. Winery manager Bertha Beringer got by selling what she could to the legal clergy and medicinal markets.

Beringer, would marry in January 1916 to Guy Young, Jr., son of a pioneer Napa ranch family, and settle down-valley with her new husband.

Charles was chosen to head the winery by his mother because of his education and good business sense. While his older brothers were quieter and more content with working in the cellars and vineyards, marrying and raising families, he was a bachelor, ambitious and outgoing. Bertha, put simply, was the oldest daughter, an excellent bookkeeper, and someone in whom her mother could have complete trust.

In essence, their work was to continue the Beringer tradition. The challenge was to hold ground . . . to make the same wines, using the same grapes and techniques inherited from their father, Jacob, against the tides of prohibition and a shrinking market. The times had changed and for the foreseeable future there would be little reason for experimentation and almost no chance for promotion and growth.

The scarcity of labor because of the World War I manpower draft added to the problems of the California wineries during the 1917 harvest. To relieve the situation, Mexican workers had to be brought in as well as several thousand Indian laborers from the Alaskan canneries. Pickers were getting $2.50 a ton that year and the market was sluggish with growers happy to get $35 a ton for their Petit Syrah. Many of them were getting very nervous about the rumors of prohibition. A statement to stockholders in March 1918 by the California Wine Association didn't help to ease the anxiety. "We don't want to be caught unready," advised M.J. Fontana, Association president. " . . for prohibition to find us with great stocks of wine on hand. We are getting ready now to be in a position to get out from under when it appears the nation is going dry."

Coming from such an influential office, the advice was ominous to Napa Valley wineries and grape men. The reaction was to look for an alternate plan. Some, like Bismark Bruck, manager of the Charles Krug winery, readied equipment to begin making non-alcoholic grape juice and extracts if prohibition really became law. Others seriously considered (and tried) grafting over their wine grape vines to black currents for making jams and jellies. For Beringer Brothers, drying the grapes seemed their most workable option.

When the full force of the Volstead Act and Prohibi-

By the beginning of the 1930s it was clear that the law abiding public wanted an end to the 18th Amendment and Prohibition.

The California wine grape industry was saved by a loophole in the 18th Amendment allowing householders to make and consume 200 gallons of "nonintoxicating" fruit juice per year. Soon growers were shipping to juice brokers like the one above in San Francisco, or sending fresh grapes by rail direct to customers who could make their own "juice."

tion struck, the Napa Valley was stunned. But it was an obscure provision in the Act permitting householders to make "nonintoxicating cider and fruit juices exclusively for use in his home" to the extent of 200 gallons yearly, that saved the vineyards. Suddenly, grape growers were inundated with orders from Eastern "grape juice" makers. Soon more "nonintoxicating" wine was being made in America's basements than the nation's wineries ever made, and the rush was on to supply the demand.

"Instead of converting their grapes into either grape juice or sacramental wines, Beringer Brothers will dry most of them," reported the *St. Helena Star* in a September 1919 edition. "The firm has just completed the installation of a Banks Fruit Evaporator and in all, forty tons of grapes have been dried. Mr. Jake Beringer says that the firm is so well pleased with the results of their experiments and with the apparent demand for dried wine grapes that it is the present intention to construct two additional units next season . . ."

For the Napa Valley vineyard owner, Prohibition just meant another crop adjustment to find the right market—a situation that had long been the story of the farmer. "There will no longer be any wine grapes in California after January 16, 1920, lamented Horatio Stoll, secretary of the California Grape Growers. " . . . the Zinfandels, Petit Syrahs, Golden Chasellas and other varieties will be used for other purposes. It will now be the object of our new publication to help growers develop a market in the Eastern states and abroad for their grape products—grape syrup, grape juice, wine grapes, dealcoholized wine, etc."

A result of the grape juice boom was that many California growers would graft over their fine Riesling, Pinot, and Cabernet vines, whose tiny, thin-skinned grapes brought them only $50 a ton, to such course, varieties as the Alicante Bouschet, which brought $100 a ton in the vineyards because it shipped and sold well.

But for most Napa Valley wineries, Prohibition was a tragedy. Many would get rid of their wine, to escape taxation, and close immediately. Others, because the law did permit wine and brandy to be made and sold for sacramental and medical purposes, would remain open on a tentative basis. It was in this latter category, rather than in shipping dried wine grapes, that Beringer Brothers found the niche that would help them survive the next decade. ❧

Most of the Beringer hillside vineyards on Spring Mountain were left to grow wild during Prohibition. Independent growers that survived this period grafted over to thick-skinned varieties that shipped well to the home "grape juice" market.

An idyllic view of Beringer winery during the dormant years of Prohibition. A footbridge above the road connects the back of the main cellar to the fermenting room.

During most of Prohibition, the winery's third floor system of belts and pulleys installed by Jacob to drive the crusher gathered cobwebs.

From 1920 to 1933 much of the winery's cooperage stood unused.

Overleaf: *The uncertainties of Prohibition caused many Napa Valley grape growers to plant other crops such as walnuts, which were in strong competition with the vineyards years after Repeal. Some survivors of those great walnut orchards stand in a field of spring mustard alongside a Beringer vineyard on Big Ranch Road.*

101

Wine Showman

Fred Abruzzini

MANY Napa Valley wineries were ruined by Prohibition, yet somehow Beringer was able to continue operating via a license to sell altar wines to the legal clergy market. But it was a low revenue operation that pushed the winery deeper in the red with each passing year. The late Jacob's daughter Bertha Beringer was doing a fine job as manager, given the fact that many of the California wineries had closed. Still, times were hard. To meet expenses and pay taxes at the height of the crisis, she would even be forced to sell off some of her valuable vineyard land along Pratt Avenue, across from the winery.

By the end of the 1920s the winery's plight would become more desperate. First came the Wall Street Crash that wrecked the nation's economy and precipitated the Great Depression. Then, in the summer of 1932, Government tax men came to the winery to deliver more bad news. In the process of measuring the contents of the wine holding tanks, they had found some serious irregularities.

It was their job under the tax codes to check the tanks at every winery, including Beringer, something they had done routinely many times in the past. But on this trip they found something suspect . . . some of the wine was missing. It was a report that devastated the always meticulous Bertha Beringer.

She was certain the problem was simply a lack of attention on the part of the cellar crew, but action had to be taken quickly. The Government men suggested she hire someone for the job with a good record for their inspections. Someone like Fred Abruzzini in the Santa Clara district.

Fred Abruzzini was the 28-year-old winemaker at Madrone Winery near San Jose. It was his uncle's operation, part of the Cribari family holdings that included the huge Cribari Winery in Fresno and other plants in New York and New Jersey. During Prohibition they were producing brandied fruits, altar wines for the clergy, and shipping fresh grapes and concentrate to home winemakers across the nation.

At Bertha's invitation, Abruzzini motored north to St. Helena to look over the job offer. "When I saw the tunnels," recalled the late winemaker in an interview at his home in Napa, "I said, Now this is a place to make wine!" The cool caves particularly impressed him because back at the Madrone operations his "aging

Young Fred Abruzzini brought a new enthusiasm to Beringer Winery during its darkest hours just before Repeal. The first outsider to ever manage the family operation, the highly motivated winemaker from Santa Clara County would become the most innovative Napa Valley promoter of the 30s and 40s. He is pictured at the winery's sales counter in 1940.

Bertha Beringer never married but devoted her years to running the winery from 1915 to 1932 when she brought in Fred Abruzzini as manager. She smiles happily with Fred's wife, Juanita, during the opening of the firm's new office in 1935.

cellar" consisted of nothing more than a large uninsulated wood barn.

Still, Abruzzini wasn't convinced that he should leave the security of his Uncle Cribari where he had worked for twelve years and "had a job for life practically." And further, since Beringer Brothers was a closely held family corporation, it wasn't likely that he would become a shareholder as promised if he stayed at Cribari.

But he finally accepted the job when the Beringers offered him the position of winery general manager, with a percentage of the profits. It was the first time in 56 years that anyone outside the family would manage the winery. Abruzzini was to be given complete control of all operations and would report to no individual family members except at the family stockholders meeting held once each year.

Just before the crush of 1932 he moved his wife Juanita and their three young sons to St. Helena and reported for work. Bertha would continue in her role as corporate Secretary while her brother Charles stayed on as President, advising from his offices in San Francisco. Their brother Otto worked in the cellar and was a stockholder, as was their sister Agnes Young who also worked occasionally at the winery. Another brother, Jacob L. Beringer, Jr., had sold his shares to the others in 1929 and left the operation.

Giving Fred Abruzzini free rein to run the winery and share in its success was one of the more fortunate Beringer decisions. For in the smiling young man from Madrone, they would soon find more than a skilled winemaker and manager but one of the most natural promoters to arrive in Napa Valley since the legendary Sam Brannan.

Within weeks he had the wine records straightened out to the satisfaction of the tax men and had turned his attention to the critical lack of cash flow, and the winery's large parcels of land lying mostly unproductive and going to weeds.

First, to get some cash coming in, he used his connections at Cribari to get more grape juice to expand altar wine sales. Then he turned his energies to the fallow land. Of real concern was the 105 acres bought some years before at the north edge of the city of Napa consisting of 55 acres planted in prunes and pears, while the rest stood barren. The Beringers were paying a man to farm the place, but were barely making enough return off the orchards to pay his salary.

The property had been on the market for years but it was the bottom of the Depression, and no one had any money. "The most we could get for the 1932 prune crop was two to three cents a pound," recalled Abruzzini. "In those days things were really bad."

There wasn't much money in sun-dried prunes but Fred had an idea. He had a carload of the fruit fancy-packed in 25 pound boxes to give out to his distributor's salesmen to use as door-openers when they called on churches to sell altar wine. Sales shot skyward and the prunes suddenly became an asset.

With the orchards now complementing the wine business, Abruzzini hired a new man to work the property on a percentage. The move proved very successful. Over the next 15 years, Beringer made money from the fruit ranch, while selling off small pieces of the land to help finance more wine-related operations.

As the years passed, land around the city of Napa became more valuable. Each parcel sold for more than the previous one, as land developers converted the Beringer property to the site of the new Wards store, several shopping centers, and residential subdivisions.

When Fred Abruzzini became manager in 1932, Beringer Brothers' total vineyard operations amounted to about 70 acres and the only grapes being crushed were mostly whites that couldn't be shipped fresh by rail to the legal home winemaker's market. All of Beringer's sweet altar wines were being bought by another winery in town, repackaged and resold and there was little market for red wine.

Looking ahead, Abruzzini decided to crush more of the 1932 crop to make dry wine and to start making Port. There was talk of repeal if Roosevelt got elected, so he bought grape concentrate from Cribari, fortified it, then blended it with some of the old Beringer's wines with good acidity. The blend would take about a year to age and by that time might be legal to sell.

It was a big gamble for Beringer Winery, but Abruzzini guessed right. Franklin D. Roosevelt was elected President in November 1932, and the outlook for the end to Prohibition seemed brighter to Napa Valley winemakers. That same month Beringer Brothers were able to capitalize on a windfall of national publicity when the $5 million American-built luxury liner *Santa Elena*, named for the city of St. Helena, was

Beringer's new office building in 1935. In recent years it has served as the winery's public relations department.

Some wines released after Repeal.

Overleaf: *With Prohibition set to end on December 5, 1933, Beringer employees mark the happy event with a portrait in front of the cellar of all the jugs, bottles, and barrels of wines they produced. Bertha Beringer is second from the right. Her sister, Martha, is in the front row, center (holding the bottle at an angle), and her sister Agnes Young is at the extreme left. Manager Fred Abruzzini is next to the worker sitting on the barrel. Office secretary Dorothea White is third from the right, seated. Others in the picture include Roy Raymond, Frederick and Arthur Beringer (Charles' sons, kneeling in the front row, left), and workers Emil Forni, Lou Mossi, and Ray Ghiringhelli.*

launched in Kearney, New Jersey. As she entered the Hackensack River, her bow was dripping with Beringer Sparkler, sent for the christening by super-promoter Fred Abruzzini.

The following year, President Roosevelt signed a law, liberalizing restrictions on medicinal wines. It may have been the signal wineries were looking for. On July 14, 1933, the *St. Helena Star* reported, "Preprohibition's days are recalled by the unusual activity at Beringer Brothers winery where ten men are at work preparing to fill the famous old winery to capacity with the present vintage.

"Fred Abruzzini, superintendent of the winery, has laid out a program of enlargement and improvement to cover a period of several years, the features of which being carried out at present are the installation of a second crusher, the re-coopering of 60 casks and the construction of a bottling building."

"By 1933 we knew Prohibition was over," said Abruzzini, "so [that year] we bought grapes from growers and we put in a new crusher. Then I got Cribari to promise delivery of 100,000 gallons of wine for 45 cents a gallon. It was December 5, 1933, when Repeal came and we were ready. We had everybody working in the bottling room."

The repeal of Prohibition meant a return to the good old days in Napa Valley. The *Star* described it in the December 8, 1933 issue: "At last, after 14 years of suspended animation, old John Barleycorn came back to life Tuesday. Beringer's famous cellars, a scene of ever increasing activity for weeks preceding Repeal, has become a madhouse. The place is swamped with work filling orders for delivery December 5th and Tuesday afternoon a procession of six enormous trucks, two of them with trailers, left Beringer Winery for points south, some heading as far as Los Angeles."

Singer Lawrence Tibbett, quoted in the national news, seemed to sum up the feelings of fellow wine buffs when he said; "I am most happy to extol the virtues of wine. It has for thousands of years been the subject of praises by all the great poets and singers. I am sure that if in the past few years we as a nation had been drinking wines instead of bootleg hard liquors, we could be a much more healthy and sober society today. So, here's to the growth and success of the glorious grape!"

For almost fifteen years the wineries had been

Paper cutouts advertising a popular red and white wine were handed out to store patrons by the thousands in the 50s.

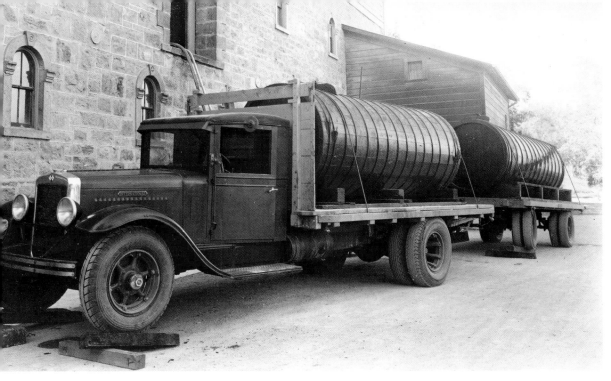

Movement of bulk juice between outside sources and the winery in the 1930s was by redwood tanks mounted on a flatbed truck and trailer. The last bit of wine was drained by running the wheels up on a makeshift ramp.

The Beringer tank truck delivering wine for blending in 1935.

A pause in the day's bottling production for a 1934 Beringer publicity shot.

Sparkling Burgundy opened a whole new market for Beringer during the 1930s and became one of their biggest sellers.

unable to sell wine. Suddenly, the boom was on and the wineries that had been closed through Prohibition were being rehabilitated with new equipment and a new optimism.

At Beringer, Fred Abruzzini, who considered himself a self-taught chemist like all the other winemakers he knew, was charged with the responsibility of getting out drinkable blends and vintages almost overnight. There were some good 1919 reds to work with, and some old 1922-23 stock for blending.

"Even Davis (University of California) didn't know wine chemistry," revealed Abruzzini about the limits of wine technology in the early 1930s. "You made alcohol and sugar and that was practically all. You didn't have to make acids. Those were done by taste. If you were a little low in acid, you'd pick out a wine that had a little higher acid."

The new demand for Beringer wines called for an updated sales organization. All through Prohibition sales and distribution to the clergy had been handled by three firms located in the east.

At the same time, Beringer president Charles "Charlie" Beringer, was running another business not associated with wine. For years he had made his home in Sausalito, within ferry commute to his office in San Francisco where he was a partner in the John P. Lynch Company soap and laundry supply business. His sister Bertha and Abruzzini now appealed to him to also take on the Beringer wholesale business, excepting for altar wines.

"He had the Beringer sales agency in San Francisco," said Abruzzini about the 1934 sales arrangement they made with Charles. "The first salesman he got was Dan Gladstone who used to sing with Al Jolson at Coffee Dan's in San Francisco.

"Right off the bat, Gladstone started selling carloads. He'd go to New Orleans and all over and sell carloads. But we couldn't fill carloads. We weren't set up for it. So I told Charlie, he's outselling us. Well that fellow didn't want to work for pennies so he went and got a job with the Guild Wine Company and made a fortune.

"Later we got Lawrence Hart who worked for Charlie out of San Francisco. He was a fellow who would sell 100 to 200 cases for smaller places . . . not agencies like Gladstone."

Oddly enough, during Prohibition demand for

Bottling room girls pose for publicity in 1935 with some new releases and a giant-size mock bottle of Sparkling Moselle. The pretty lass at the right is Ramona Gooden, soon to be the bride of Otto, Jr., "Tiny" Beringer. Their son Fred is co-producer of this book.

In May, 1934, Beringer became the first Napa Valley winery to open to the public, thus beginning the area's wine tourist business. That September, manager Fred Abruzzini (foreground, in white sport coat) would test his innovative idea to the extreme when his invitation brought 5,000 overflow visitors who strolled over from St. Helena's Vintage Festival celebration. Reported the St. Helena Star, "The good-natured merry-makers waited patiently in line and entered the winery two-abreast, signing registers. They were then permitted to pass through the underground cellars dug into the hillside. When they completed the inspection, they landed at a long service table where a number of employees asked them to choose the dry or sweet wine they preferred . . . And somehow they found that the wine tasted better when sipped in a cool cellar that has a vinous smell, with huge carved oval oak casks . . ."

Cheered by their trademark jugs of "White in the morning" and "Red in the afternoon," Beringer revelers demonstrate the art of making wine. Their float was an entry in the St. Helena Vintage Festival, an annual event revived after Prohibition. The three- day celebration featured a big Labor Day parade, wine pageant, carnival, and nightly open air dancing, bringing thousands by train from the San Francisco Bay area.

Beringer's 1935 entry in the St. Helena Vintage Festival parade.

Contestants in the 1934 St. Helena Vintage Festival wine barrel race. The winner was Roy Raymond from Beringer.

grapes for home winemaking actually increased California's wine grape acreage by 112 percent over a ten year period. Napa Valley vineyards didn't really fare that badly and with the return of the wineries as customers, it was time for a celebration. In September 1934, St. Helena marked repeal of the 18th Amendment by holding its first Vintage Festival since 1919.

"Besides the pageant there will be a huge exhibit tent filled with displays of wine grapes and wine making equipment of today and of the days gone by," reported the *St. Helena Star*. "There will be carnival attractions, open air dancing, band concerts, and a spectacular Labor Day parade. Open house during the event will be held at Beringer Brothers, Greystone, and Beaulieu cellars . . ."

Beringer Winery was situated perfectly for the overflow crowds from the festival and all the attendant publicity. The winery was within walking distance at the edge of town, and Fred Abruzzini was so proud of the Beringer's aging caves that in May he had opened them to visitors for tours—the first Napa Valley winery to open to the mass public.

Business was definitely looking up by the summer of 1935, so Beringer Winery announced plans for a major expansion. "I was getting wine on thirty, sixty, ninety day trade acceptance from Cribari," reminisced Abruzzini. "Until 1935 we had no sweet wines (made by Beringer) at all. We had to buy everything from Cribari. We were crushing our grapes making dry wines. So we made enough money with Cribari by 1935 to start the buildings."

Fred Abruzzini, together with Bertha and Charles Beringer and a big help from Repeal, turned the winery around. Cash flow had improved enough to enable them to take out a construction loan to expand and improve the plant.

By the start of the 1935 crush Beringer had replaced the old fermenting room with a new one, constructed a new office, installed new redwood storage tanks, two new hydraulic presses, and built a new barrel room with cooperage enough for 200,000 gallons.

Learning the wine trade during this period were two young men who would play major roles in the future of Beringer Winery. Otto Jr. ("Tiny") Beringer was a blonde giant who excelled at sports, attended Stanford and then came home to work at the family winery. The timing was right, since his father, Otto Sr.,

Housewives, like these women picking at Beringer's in 1935, supplemented local labor in the Napa Valley during the Depression. By the end of WWII, migrant Mexican help predominated.

Before tractors came on the scene, horses worked the vineyards. Beringer winery kept several of the animals until well after the fuel shortages of WWII, using them mostly on the hillsides. In this hand-tinted 1937 promotional slide a team is pictured on Spring Mountain bringing in the grape harvest.

Skidding a load of Beringer grapes out of the vineyard by horse team.

For many years the standard grape picking container for California vineyards was the 32-pound wood fruit box or "lug." Later in the 1960s came the plastic "tray" in use now. Workers pick into it, then toss the contents into an open "gondola" trailer which can be quickly transported to the crusher.

Dumping grapes into the crusher conveyer in the 1950's.

A 1935 experiment in bringing grapes to the winery in open bins.

121

son of the original founder, Jacob Beringer, was considering retiring as cellar foreman.

The other young man was Otto's friend, Roy Raymond, a powerful athlete from Marin county who once swam the Golden Gate. Roy was a good friend of Charles Beringer's son Arthur, and after leaving high school in 1933 took a summer job at the winery at 40 cents and hour, the standard wage at that time for laborers. He liked winery life enought to make it his career, mastering all aspects of the business while finding time to marry Otto's sister, Martha Jane.

Following Repeal, between 1933 and 1935, there were a lot of new vineyards planted in the Napa Valley. By 1938, when they all came into production, the struggling industry suffered because of over production. It was simply a case of too much wine, too many grapes and few buyers.

Napa Valley was not alone, all of the state's vineyards were suffering from a surplus of grapes. So it was decided that the California wineries would have to go on a pro-rated formula whereby a percentage of all the crush that year would go into brandy.

Several wineries in the valley had stills but none that could turn out the 190-proof brandy that Beringer was capable of producing on their new equipment. Recalled Abruzzini, "We had the distillery, but in those days Christian Brothers had the big brandy business. They were the brandy kings."

Then suddenly, the Beringer distillery was much in demand making custom brandy for such wineries as Beaulieu Vineyards, St. Helena Co-op and Christian Brothers. With this operation now running full steam the money began rolling in.

Prohibition had left the valley vineyards in a shambles. It wasn't until about 1940 that the Napa growers began concentrating on quality. Up to that time Beringer Winery had about 70 acres planted in Golden Chasselas, Green Hungarian, Semillon, Riesling, Cabernet Sauvignon and Black Pinot.

"After Prohibition people liked their wines real heavy," remembers Roy Raymond. "They got (from the wineries) a red wine that you could cut with a knife. Lots of flavor and lots of body to them. Your pets (Petite Sirahs) were a pretty good source of supply throughout the whole valley and made a pretty gutty wine. They (the wineries) fermented everything dry on the skins, and aged them longer as a general rule."

Roy Raymond, left, and his giant pal Otto, Jr., "Tiny" Beringer in 1934. Both were fine athletes but made their careers the Beringer wine business . . . Roy in the cellars, and Otto in the vineyards. Roy married Otto's sister, Martha Jane, and in the end the two families were the last of the Beringer descendents to operate the winery.

Hard working and likeable, Roy Raymond blends wine in 1934. He stayed on to run the cellar and marry a Beringer girl.

The winery as it appeared in 1936, with vineyard on both sides of the highway and the horse barn in the foreground. During this time the Rhine House and its grounds, left, belonged to the Booth family.

The barrel room of the stone cellar building as it appeared in the 1940s.

Once the wine is placed in barrels to age it still requires a close watch to maintain quality. During the Abruzzini years Beringer cellarmen made the rounds every Monday, filling the cooperage to the top to replace what had leaked or evaporated, so the trapped air would not spoil the valuable contents. After three months the wine was transferred into large tanks for blending, then back to the smaller barrels for another three months of aging. This process was kept up for four years before the wine was ready for market.

A Beringer cellarman checks a Cabernet for clarity in 1938.

Fred Abruzzini (on ladder) tops wine barrels stored in the cool aging caves.

It was in 1940 that the Beringer vineyard across the highway from the winery was replanted to upgrade quality. For years, the vineyard was planted to a "field blend," mixture of Cabernet Sauvignon, Petite Sirah, Carignane, Zinfandel and some Pinot Noir. In other words, according to Raymond, "interplanted to thirteen vines of Cabernet Sauvignon, twenty of Carignane, fifteen of Petite Sirah, etc., in the same row."

The idea was to make the blends in the vineyard to save time and expense in the winery. But in practice, wine quality was difficult to obtain because the grapes ripened and reached their peaks at different times.

For the new vineyard the winery would plant in traditional style separate blocks of Cabernet Sauvignon, French Colombard, Johannisberg Riesling, Malvasia Bianca and Early Burgundy.

Since Prohibition, Beringer had been buying some grape juice for brandy-making from Eschol Winery near Napa (now Trefethen). When Eschol owner Clark Fawver died in 1940, Fred Abruzzini negotiated a long-term lease with his widow to operate the extensive vineyards and winery as part of expanded Beringer operations. It was an important addition that would help assure a source of quality grapes for the forseeable future. Meanwhile Agnes Young, Jacob's daughter and Beringer stockholder, would make her residence there when the widow Fawver moved away.

At the outbreak of World War II, many California wineries would begin shipping wine to countries whose supply was shut off by the chaos in Europe.

"We had a lot of wine at that time," recalls Roy Raymond. "We were selling a lot of red wine to China just prior to the war years. I guess the French had run into their problems in Europe with Hitler's rise and all the troubles before the United States got into the war.

"I don't recall how long this went on . . . I think probably a year and a half or so. You know at that time the French Army was on a wine ration. It was supplied to them as part of the daily diet."

When the United States entered World War II, the main impact on the California wine industry was that bottles and capsules, corks and foil became scarce. Foil capsules came from England, corks from Spain and Portugal. Alarmed by the scarcity, Fred Abruzzini helped initiate an action to get the State Forestry to plant cork oak trees in the Napa Valley.

Abruzzini's idea, however, wouldn't help the

Hand corking bottles of wine at Beringer in 1940.

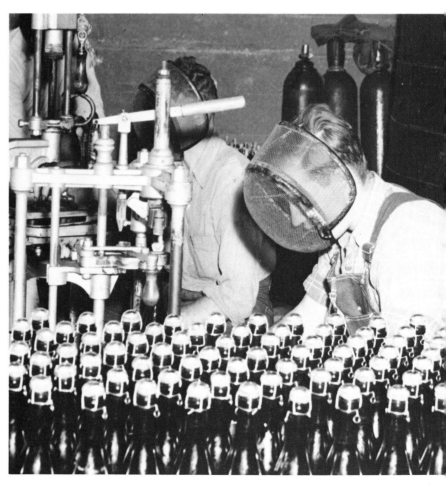
Masked to cork volatile sparkling wine.

A worker operates the labeling and foiling machine in the bottling room. By 1940, Beringer was selling about 40,000 cases of wine a year, a respectable figure for the time.

Fred Abruzzini inspects newly bottled wine. Once corked and labeled, the bottles were laid on slats in huge banks. This was to keep the cork wet and expanded, to keep out intruding air. The wine was kept in this manner from six months to two years for mellowing.

130

1946 sales brochure

immediate shortage since it took a long time to grow a tree that could be stripped of its useful bark every eight years. Many state-sponsored trees were planted but in the end it proved far too expensive to start a cork oak tree industry in California, so alternatives were found until the end of the war when the European cork supply could be resumed.

The war on the home-front seemed an eternity to Beringer. There was a shortage of fuel and tires to keep the trucks running, and a shortage of men to prune the vineyards and pick the crops. But the hard times helped unite the community. Beringer employees even joined in with the national crusade and planted their own "victory garden" on the winery grounds. Here, at lunch-time and after work, they tended the vegetable rows to help with the general scarcity of food on the store shelves.

Unlike the days of Prohibition, producing California wineries were now considered essential to the well-being of the nation. Not only were they providing a product that was common to many American dinner tables, but the making of wine was also helping with the war effort.

Tartrates from the waste grape skins and stems, and from the wine lees and argols, were used in the manufacture of rayon for tents and parachutes and in the making of some medicines. Cream of tartar, another by-product, found widespread use in a variety of ways.

The labor shortage during World War II was a problem for all U.S. agriculture, as well as the wine industry. Sailors on leave from nearby Mare Island, and Army Air Corpsman from Travis and Hamilton Field proved to be the best grape pickers Beringer could find. The winery was so desperate one harvest season that they even tried a busload of inmates from the local mental hospital.

California's wine industry flourished after the war, partly because of the heavy damage sustained to the best vineyards and cellars of France and the Rhineland.

To meet the opportunity for new markets, Beringer Winery expanded in 1951 by purchasing the Garetto Winery in the Carneros district at the south end of Napa Valley. Acquisition of this plant increased the St. Helena winery's capacity to two million gallons and its vineyard lands to 600 acres. It was a move calculated to position Beringer for whatever lay ahead in what was rapidly becoming the post-War boom. ❧

A window display card from the 1940-50s Beringer advertising campaigns.

Despite the shortage of bottles and corks during WWII, Beringer

Winery found a way to stay in business. Fred Abruzzini (behind map) and some of his employees show what they have to offer in 1942.

After World War II Beringer continued to be one of the most visited winerys in Napa Valley. In 1951, when General Electric held a dealer convention in San Francisco 60 busloads came for a tour. Here some of the GE people in theme western hats line up outside the cellars.

In the years when regular passenger service ran through Napa Valley, tourists often came by rail to visit the wineries. Beringer trucks are pictured picking up a large group of San Francisco Guardsmen who came on an outing to St. Helena in June 1951. The Guardsmen were composed of prominent businessmen who worked with underpriviledged youth.

Keeping up with the demand of the post-War boom, Beringer Winery began buying more grapes from outside vineyards. Manager Fred Abruzzini is shown in 1948 checking some Cabernet Sauvignon brought in by grower Marco Calleri to be processed by a new stainless steel crusher that could handle sixty tons per hour.

Chardonnay ready for harvest.

From the time he left Stanford to make his career with the family-owned winery, Otto "Tiny" Beringer managed the vineyards and equipment. A massive man, with a good sense of humor, he was being prepared to one day take over the business.

Overleaf: *A Beringer vineyard beyond Calistoga in Knights Valley. The winery first developed land to grow grapes here under Otto Beringer's management. Today, it produces some of the best wines.*

The Celebrities

IT was Fred Abruzzini who first recognized the potential of promoting the old stone cellars and cool aging tunnels of Beringer as a showplace for visitors.

The new manager was a natural publicist and in April, 1934, would startle the Napa Valley vintners by being the first to open his winery to public tours. Except on special occasions, there would be no free tastings but visitors were taken on a guided walk through the moss-covered tunnels and during the fall season could observe how the grapes were brought in and crushed. The tour ended at a sales counter where they could buy the Beringer wine of their choice.

Back in the 1920s, when he worked briefly as a truck driver, Abruzzini met cowboy movie star Tom Mix when he was making a film at a ranch near San Francisco. Mix hired him as an extra in the production and from that day on the winemaker would have a lifelong interest in famous personalities.

Later, while working with Cribari winery during Prohibition, he sold the firm's Sunny Boy-brand dried fruit to Young's Market in Hollywood where all the stars shopped. He met some of the celebrities and when he took the job at Beringer, began inviting them up. "The thing that really got them interested," said the late winemaker, "was when radio personality Jane Lee began talking about us. I took her picture in front of our big carved barrel, then framed it and hung it there. Right away the publicity men started coming. I told them I could do more advertising for their stars with those pictures than they could."

The Vintage Festival held in St. Helena in 1935 gave another boost to Beringer winery's new image as northern California's "in" place for celebrities. Abruzzini's old friend Tom Mix brought his traveling circus to town as part of the entertainment and later took a tour of Beringer. Heavyweight boxing champ Max Baer had relatives in town and also came by to put his signature in Fred's new guest register book.

Abruzzini made sure that both the local and Hollywood newspapers reported these events, and the publicity began snowballing. Soon every movie star, media personality, diplomat and politician visiting the San Francisco Bay area seemed to be including a stop at Beringer winery as part of their itinerary.

The 1939 Golden Gate Exposition held on man-made Treasure Island in San Francisco Bay brought thousands to the area and Abruzzini saw this as a real opportunity. He had a colorful map produced showing "the main highways to Beringer Bros. Winery and other interesting points . . ." Every evening after closing the cellars, he would bundle his wife Juanita and three young sons in the family car and drive the 60 miles to the fair. There they would stand outside the gates handing out the maps. The next morning a sizeable crowd of visitors would be waiting at the winery to take a tour.

Fred Abruzzini also passed out maps at the Golden Gate Theatre in San Francisco. From this promotion, Hollywood scout Lou Shapiro visited the winery one day in 1940 while looking for a location for a proposed film titled *They Knew What They Wanted*. The story was based on the Napa Valley and required a winery setting, as well as an old farmhouse and vineyard. Shapiro fell for the beauty of Beringer's as his winery set and chose the Fagani ranch on Oakville Road for the ranch scenes. The nearby train depot in Oakville also played a part in the picture.

The star of the film was Carole Lombard, the sexy

Under Fred Abruzzini's management, Beringer Winery would be the first in Napa Valley to open for tours. His brand of publicity would also attract many famous visitors. Here he signs in actor Charles Laughton who was at the winery for the 1940 filming of They Knew What They Wanted.

blonde actress recently wed to screen idol Clark Gable. "Upper Napa Valley was nearly turned upside down when she arrived by train in St. Helena for the filming," Abruzzini remembered vividly. "Gable was making a picture in Chile at the time. He visited her later on the set and they had a big birthday party for him at the St. Helena Hotel."

Carole Lombard was soon photographed in front of the now-famous Beringer Winery carved barrel. Her picture too was tacked onto the barrel's growing gallery. Other important visitors wanted their pictures taken and before long Abruzzini had installed a big Speed Graphic camera on a tripod behind the door, ready for the next celebrity that dropped in.

By 1940 more than 25,000 people were visiting Beringer Winery yearly. The regular public was always invited, but now with all the publicity about celebrity visitors, companys and social clubs began coming to the grounds for their annual picnics. The Fuller Paint Company group, especially, came every year. It helped that the Fuller family summer home was just a block away down Main Street.

During the travel restrictions of World War II, winery visitation dropped off to a trickle but still a few noteworthy people came by. In 1945 former world boxing champion Jack Dempsey visited in uniform while on a recruitment drive for the National Guard. Actress Ginger Rogers began making Beringer a regular stop whenever she made the trip north to visit her mother in Oregon. Military officers, admirals, generals, and civilian government officials from Bay Area offices would also find relaxation in a trip to St. Helena and Beringer Winery.

After the War, Beringer Winery would gain worldwide exposure for its fine wine and hospitality during the United Nations Conference held in San Francisco. Diplomats and their staffs found the winery charming and gracious.

By this time, the famous old Rhine House mansion which had been sold to outside parties, was back in the ownership of the Beringer family and winery. Barbecues and picnics were now being held on the grounds nearly every weekend by one large group or another and a staff of seasoned guides were conducting hourly tours through the famous wine tunnels.

Max Baer, who had gone into acting, had his own Sunday radio show broadcasting from the Cliff House

in San Francisco. He gave publicity a big boost by signing off with . . . "Now I'm going up to Beringer winery and see Fred Abruzzini." He meant it too, and visited the winery so much in the 1950s that he was considered something of the official mascot. "We'd have lunch at the Valley Coffee Shop [in St. Helena]," reminisced Abruzzini. "Max would always give any kids he saw on the street a dollar apiece. He was a great sport."

But of all the stars who visited the winery through the years, none was a bigger connoisseur of Beringer wine than crooner Rudy Vallee. The amiable singer-actor boosted it widely among his friends and came regularly to stock up on vintages for his renowned private cellar.

The winery has continued to attract celebrities. In 1956 R.K.O. Pictures filmed *Unholy Wife* here, starring Rod Steiger and British actress Diana Dors. In 1959 Universal shot scenes here also for *This Earth is Mine*, starring Rock Hudson. In recent years, the Rhine House has been very popular with camera crews as one of the best backdrops in California's wine country.

What all the earlier publicity from famous visitors did for Beringer winery would be hard to measure in dollars and cents. Certainly it increased its popularity. But what Abruzzini's promotions did for Napa Valley was to put it on the map as a place to visit. By the time he retired in 1956, all of the major wineries were not only conducting public tours and tastings but were basking in the glory as being part of one of the best known, most beautiful wine-producing regions of the world. ❧

Some of the celebrities who have visited Beringer Winery:

singer, Louis Armstrong	*actor*, Peter Graves
actor, Don Ameche	*Gov.* Earl Warren
boxer, Gene Tunney	*actor*, Ed Wynn
actor, Jack Oakie	*actress*, Merle Oberon
actress, Dorothy Lamour	*cowboy singer*, Roy Rogers
comedians, Bud Abbott	*circus star*, Clyde Beatty
and Lou Costello	*actor*, George Peppard
ventriloquist, Edgar Bergen	*actor*, Ronald Coleman
boxer, Rocky Marciano	*baseball player*, Mel Ott
actor, Joe E. Brown	*actor*, Charles Coburn

Opposite page: Abruzzini's 1939 map

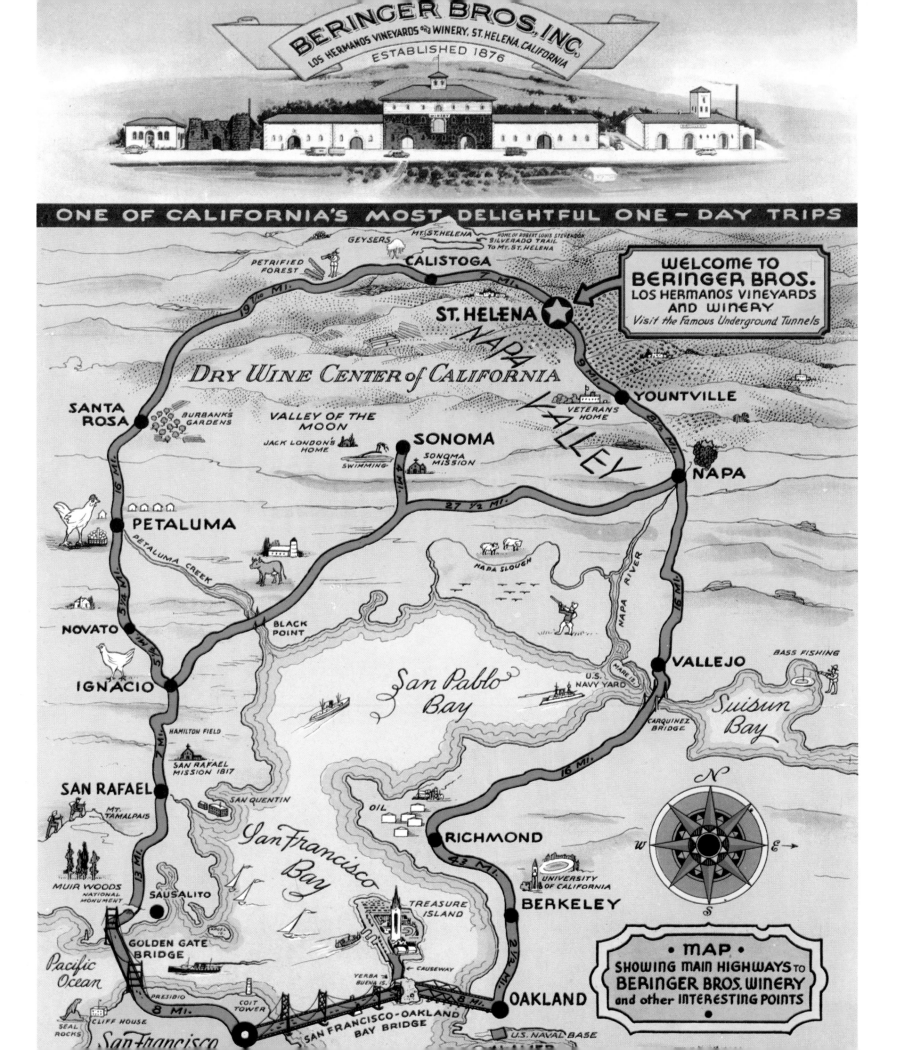

Garson Kanin, Carole Lombard and winery manager Fred Abruzzini tour the Beringer aging cellars in 1940.

Hollywood stars Charles Laughton and Carole Lombard making wine selections at Beringer.

Carole Lombard uses a "wine thief" to sample a vintage from a Beringer barrel. With her is Garson Kanin, director of the 1940 film "They Knew What They Wanted." At the peak of her career, Lombard would make two more films, and then lose her life tragically January 16, 1942, in a plane crash while touring the country on a drive to sell Defense Bonds. Two years later when the Liberty ship "Carole Lombard" was launched, it was christened with a bottle of Beringer "Sparkler" swung by her good friend Irene Dunne, as her heart-broken husband Capt. Clark Gable of the U.S. Army Air Force saluted.

145

One of the Beringer gift packs selected by Carole Lombard "Gable" during her visit in 1940, and the check for her purchases.

Ventriloquist Edgar Bergen, of "Charlie McCarthy" radio fame, pours a glass of Beringer Chablis for his secretary Mary Hanrahan at St. Gothard's restaurant in St. Helena. Bergen was visiting in 1948 with his RKO publicity director and was a house guest of Misses Bertha and Martha Beringer at their home on the winery grounds.

Clark Gable's Packard convertible is pictured at Beringer winery during a visit in 1940. The Napa Valley so impressed him that after WWII he came back several times a year. A good friend from southern California, Al Menasco, bought a ranch in St. Helena and in 1955 Gable and his new bride Kay Spreckels honeymooned here and took a tour of the Beringer cellars.

Screen idol Clark Gable and his old friend Fred Abruzzini during a visit to the winery in 1955.

Ben Alexander, star of the "Dragnet" TV series, actress Lenore Stern, and character actor Charles Coburn pose with manager Fred Abruzzini in 1955 in front of the famed Beringer carved barrel with its gallery of celebrity photos.

Stars Rod Steiger and Diana Dors rehearse a Beringer cellar scene from the 1956 film "Unholy Wife". A favorite Napa Valley movie location, the winery also played a role in the 1959 shooting of "This Earth is Mine" starring Rock Hudson and Jean Simmons.

Former world heavyweight boxing champ and film actor Max Baer hams it up with Beringer guests at the outside tasting bar in 1953. Baer, whose screen credits include the 1933 film "Prizefighter and the Lady," had relatives in St. Helena and was a winery regular for nearly thirty years.

Overleaf: *Chabot Vineyard, after harvest, begins to take on fall colors. Set along the gentle slopes of Glass Mountain, its Cabernet Sauvignon would become a modern Beringer classic.*

151

After more than two decades the winery was under full family control again. President Bertha Beringer is pictured in 1956 with her nephew Otto Beringer, right, and his brother-in-law and new assistant Roy Raymond.

Family Vintners

Otto and Roy

*B*ERINGER Winery marked its 80th anniversary in 1956 and in July Fred Abruzzini retired after 24 years as winemaker and manager. He had directed it with style and imagination through the lean days of the Depression and world war, and brought it new fame and glory. But it was time to take a bow and let the Beringer family run their own show.

As the years went by, the winery's ownership had passed to Jacob's four surviving children, Otto, Bertha, Martha and Agnes, and the widow of their late brother Charles. Charles Beringer, who had served as winery president for 40 years, died in 1955 and Bertha had taken over the mostly honorary role. All were well along in age, Bertha and Martha had never married, Agnes had no offspring, and between the brothers only Otto had a surviving son to carry on the name. Fortunately, Otto had two children, Otto Jr. and Martha Jane, and it was on their shoulders that rode all the family's hope for the future.

Big Otto Beringer Jr. cut his teeth on a grape box and grew up doing chores around the winery. After an impressive athletic record at St. Helena High and a stint at Stanford he took over as Beringer vineyard manager in the mid-1930s and had become a seasoned veteran of the business. A bear of a man, but gentle, he was well-liked by his aunts and so it was no surprise to St. Helena when he was named Abruzzini's successor.

His new assistant would be his brother-in-law Roy Raymond who started with the winery in 1933, married Otto's sister Martha Jane in 1936, and had put in twenty years at Beringer as cellar master. It was a good match. The two men had been close friends since their youth and could work as a team. Otto would handle the office, public relations and marketing and Roy would run the rest of the operation as winemaker. A popular member of the St. Helena City Council, Roy was also good in dealing with community affairs.

They took over in the booming 1950s. Lucky for them, per-capita wine consumption in the United States was soaring. Millions were discovering wine as a symbol of status and culture, people were taking up gourmet cooking with it, and housewives were beginning to serve wine with the family dinner.

At the same time, Americans suddenly had more leisure time and their habits were changing fast. In trendy California, people out for a Sunday or weekend drive were becoming more destination-oriented and not only expected to explore and be entertained when they got there, but were willing to leave some money. The Napa Valley wineries were changing too, adjusting to the new wave of tourism as a good way to boost the popularity and sale of their wines. All of the most successful ones like Martini, Inglenook, and Krug had an interesting history, quite often a legendary family

Well-kept and prosperous, Beringer Winery is pictured in the summer of 1958.

head or winemaker, and always a guided tour of the cellars and grounds, and a free wine tasting.

Tourism had become a force and the winery that had all the right elements of history, setting, and good wine was bound to attract the most attention.

Beringer Winery seemed to have the edge, including colorful characters; like former boxing champ Max Baer who had become something of a regular glad-hander; old Manuel the meticulous gardener; and the debonair guides who were often retired actors or writers who charmed the visitors with their wit and wine talk. Even the spinster Beringer sisters, Bertha and Martha, who lived on the grounds in the old farm house added something to the legend. They kept to themselves, yet had a swimming pool, a big car, and a houseboy named Tommy who was an ex-lightweight boxer, marvelous cook and comic gad-about.

The historic limestone tunnels were another Beringer plus. No other major Napa Valley winery had such an irresistible attraction.

Beringer also had the Rhine House and one of the first actions taken by Otto and Roy as managers was to put the spotlight on the elegant old mansion as their main center of attention. It had stood empty for years and now work was begun to bring it back to all its old splendor. Dense shrubbery that obscured the place was cut back to open Frederick's beautiful old home and gardens to the highway out front, the interior was refurbished, and in late 1956 the Rhine House was opened to the public as the winery's hospitality center.

The ambience was now nearly complete. Opening the mansion gave visitors a place to linger and explore after the tour of the cellars, enjoying the architecture of the fine old home while sampling some of the Beringer vintages at the new tasting area set up in one of the beautifully panelled rooms. Guides were more professional in explaining the different wines which could be purchased at a good price in the new retail room and gift shop.

"The picture-book effect of formal flower beds and sloping expanses of lawns," reported the *Napa Register* in a 1958 article, "and the three-story gabled house built in 1883, is part of a summer tour that Napa Valley residents may be assured is equal to any sight-seeing attraction in the Bay Area. A chat with a tourist contingent from the East, summarized their visit to Rhine House as a highlight of the wine-growing country."

157

By the late 1950s there were five major wineries besides Beringer competing for the wine tourist; Inglenook, Beaulieu, Louis Martini, Charles Krug and Christian Brothers. All of these old cellars had interesting tours. Now, more than ever, the emphasis would be on turning out the better wine.

Otto and Roy decided to reintroduce an old Beringer wine called Barenblut ("bear's blood"), a pleasing blend of Grignolino and Pinot Noir. It wasn't for everyone but it gave them something different. They made other changes in their premium line as well.

"Popular tastes in wine have changed a lot," Otto noted in 1959. "Consumers today favor the light-bodied vintages to the heavier wines preferred before. Rosé wines have become very popular and there is more interest today, perhaps due to so many Americans traveling abroad."

To meet the growing competition, Otto and Roy stepped up the pace to upgrade their vineyards. They bought land in Knights Valley, 17 miles north of the winery, cleared it and planted Pinot Noir, Cabernet Sauvignon, Chardonnay and Chenin Blanc. Another large tract was purchased south on Yountville Crossroad and planted to premium varietals.

By now the next generation of Beringers would pitch in to help with the work. Roy Raymond's two sons were the first in the family to study wine in college. Roy Jr. came home with a degree in viticulture and was made manager of the vineyards. His younger brother Walter would soon get a degree in enology and begin working with his father to refine the quality of the wines.

Young Fred Beringer, Otto's son, went to work in the sales department. His job was to get out on the road to learn what the consumer wanted and what sold best in the stores. The popular wines in the early '60s were the Chenin Blancs and the Vin Rose's, light wines that went well with everything from afternoon parties to picnics and social events.

But varietals were capturing more interest and the Beringers realized that here lay their real destiny. Fine premium wines were what they had spent nearly a century developing a reputation for and they had always been at the forefront producing to meet the consumers's taste. Now, as the market wanted more quality, they would renew efforts to make their Chardonnays and Cabernet Sauvignons the best sellers.

Little changed from Jacob and Frederick's day, the bottling room in 1957 still required a lot of hand labor. Automation was yet to come.

Opposite: *Beringer winemaker Roy Raymond inspects some early vintages stored in the cellar.*

Managing the winery had its rewards. Otto Beringer takes time in 1957 to pose with a bevy of visiting beauties from the Miss Universe pageant. Left to right are, Miss Cuba, Miss Venezuela, Miss Costa Rica, and Miss San Francisco.

A giant wine glass attracts attention at a 1958 Beringer promotion.

The increased interest in Napa Valley wines during the 1960s brought a new sophistication as visitors wanted to learn every detail. Here a Beringer staff member explains a Chenin Blanc at a benefit tasting in 1966.

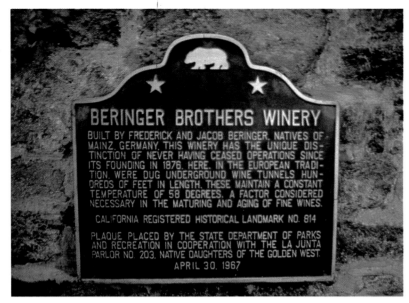

Highlight of 1967 was the naming of the 91-year-old Beringer
Winery as a State Historical Landmark. Family descendents
Fred Beringer (son of Otto Jr.) and Craig Raymond (son of
Roy Raymond Jr.) did the unveiling.

Fred Beringer helps unveil the special bronze marker during
1967 ceremonies.

Native Daughters of the Golden West and Beringer family members at the winery's historical dedication.

Otto and Roy continued to build the winery's business through the end of the 1960s, when a series of events suddenly shook Beringer Winery to its stone foundations. First, rumors that their land in Knights Valley would be the site of a proposed new lake forced them to overextend in their purchase of alternative land in Yountville. Then, in 1968, after spending thousands to plant the big Yountville property, a disastrous spring frost damaged the vines. The vineyards were equipped with the latest sprinkler system for frost protection but thirty straight nights of freezing temperatures used up all their pond water and the young vines were badly burned.

It was a real setback but the worst was yet to come. One by one, Jacob Beringer's elderly sons and daughters were dying and the estate was being burdened with inheritance taxes. After Charles, Otto Sr. died in 1960, Agnes awhile later, Martha in 1969, and Bertha, the last of them, in 1970.

Bertha's death forced a decision. Whether to borrow money to pay the taxes and put in the new vineyards and winery equipment necessary to stay competitive, or sell out.

"The inheritance tax factor dictated that we had to sell," says Roy Raymond who has since been honored among his peers as a Napa Valley "Legend of Wine." "We sold to Néstle. Really, as far as Beringer was concerned it was the best answer. Changes were beginning to happen in the industry. Quality was increasing every year and so much of it was dependent on new equipment and we just didn't have the money."

A great dynasty had come to an end. In settling the estate the entire Beringer property, including 700 acres of vineyards, was sold in 1971 to Néstle the famous Swiss maker of quality food products, which was branching out into premium wine. The reported sale price was $6 million.

But the story doesn't end with the Beringer's fading quietly away to history. A new chapter in this family of winemakers is being written today by Jacob's great grandsons, Roy Raymond Jr. and his brother Walter. With their father's help, they have plowed their part of the inheritance back into the land—creating new vineyards in St. Helena and building Raymond Winery from the ground up. Wine is in their blood and they are carrying on the traditions in a way that would make all the old Beringers proud. ❧

It was the death of Bertha Beringer in 1970, after all of her brothers and sisters had passed away, that compelled the heirs to sell the winery property because of the huge tangle of inheritance taxes. The last of her generation of Beringers, she is pictured, left, with her sister Martha in the gardens of their home on the winery grounds where they lived out their lives as spinsters.

Overleaf: *Looking west across a section of the Gamble Ranch vineyard near Oakville. After Beringer's sale to Néstle, Chardonnay from here would help establish a new super-premium wine program.*

A Napa Valley Legend

Beringer

TODAY, Beringer is one of the most famous names in premium wine. How it earned its place among the very best is a story of the imagination, dedication to excellence, and great patience of many visionary people.

At the time Néstle company purchased the historic old winery and its vineyards from the heirs of the founders in 1971, there were significant changes taking place in the Napa Valley. Internationally, wine consumers, wine makers and wine growers had acknowledged the excellence of wines produced here. With this recognition came a new renaissance as the region's old established wineries and prime vineyard lands suddenly came into demand. Many of Europe's most established names in wine and food began investing in the valley. Néstle, already renowned for its fine food products, was looking for the right property to begin producing premium California wine and when Beringer winery and vineyards came on the market, it was ideal.

But before the stately old St. Helena landmark could become a modern premium operation, it would need a complete refurbishing. Néstle had made the

The fifth Beringer wine-maker in one hundred years, stepping in for the new owners, was Myron Nightingale who arrived in 1971. Architect of a new premium wine masterplan, he would achieve spectacular results and many awards before retiring in 1984 as consulting Winemaster Emeritus.

Myron Nightingale

Fine Cabernet rests in the restored limestone tunnels.

The handsome old cellar buildings and deep tunnels, which were extensively renovated by Wine World in the mid-1970s, continue the time-honored tradition of wood-aging fine Beringer wines.

investment for the long term and the first priority soon after the Beringer purchase was to select a veteran winemaker thoroughly familiar with California's soils and climate, with one objective—to produce world-class wines. The position required someone who was already a master, who had style and imagination.

The company found the qualities it was looking for in Myron Nightingale, the highly-respected winemaker for the Cresta Blanca brand where he had become widely acclaimed for his experiments with induced Botrytis—*pourriture noble*— which was used to make a superior sweet wine called *Premier Sémillon.* Something of a living winemaking legend, Nightingale was a graduate of the University of California in 1940, a member of that distinguished group now known as the "Great Winemaker's Class."

Through the years Nightingale had worked with almost every grape variety that grew in California. He was known for his attention to detail and dedication to quality, and if those weren't credentials enough—his dream had always been to do his work in the Napa Valley.

Nightingale accepted the position at Beringer and was made "winemaster." He was given free rein to take whatever action was needed to initiate a super-premium wine program and began by assessing the equipment. One look at the cellar's ancient cooperage, much of it nearly 40 years old, and he knew that this was the place to start. To have full control over the quality he wanted, these old relics of a bygone era would have to go.

His first action was to begin a selective process of installing temperature-controlled fermentation tanks and replacing the old cooperage with fresh new French oak barrels.

The new owners saw great promise and beauty in the historic old winery and started at once restoring it to its original condition. Nearly a century of weathering and earthquakes had taken their toll to the large stone building and its underground tunnels and it would take months of careful engineering and craftsmanship to renew the cellars for winemaking.

An interesting highlight of this work in late January, 1973, was the surprise discovery of the original cellar cornerstone with "1877" carved on its face. When it was officially opened a few days later, its chamber revealed some old papers inside a sherry

Beringer winemaster Ed Sbragia polished his skills as an enologist working with Myron Nightingale on the "reserve" and "experimental" programs. He has set new standards of excellence with his wines by constantly refining to realize the fullest potential from each vineyard.

After years of dedication to detail by Wine World, Beringer wines have achieved world-class status. A panel of tasters judge a new vintage in the ambience of the Rhine House gardens.

bottle and six coins, including a valuable 1807 Liberty silver dollar. The find would spark an idea for a future winery museum envisioned to display other historic artifacts associated with the property and winemaking in the Napa Valley.

While the cellar work was underway, it was decided to make the old Beringer estate into a model visitor center that would give guests a more memorable Napa Valley experience. Plans were carried out to renovate the 17-room Rhine House, with the main floor reserved for wine tasting and the gift shop. The upper level now houses private tasting rooms and the Founder's Room where limited and older bottlings are available to the public for sampling and sale. The new landscape design tied the mansions with foot paths to the old cellar buildings and aging tunnels where expertly guided tours are now conducted continually throughout the day.

It proved to be just what small, intimate groups wanted—a place where they could come and enjoy a glass of wine and browse one of the valley's fine old homes and gardens. The beautifully restored Rhine House and tunnels also provided the perfect introduction to wine novices without intimidating them.

Myron Nightingale was a firm believer in the old maxim that, "great wines are made in the vineyard. They are a joint venture between the winemaker and grower." With this as his rule, the Beringer winemaster began augmenting his work with the cellar facilities by upgrading his vineyards to get the best premium varietals possible.

In the beginning, he would have as vineyard manager Roy Raymond Jr., who continued on for a few years after his family sold the property. Together they started developing a new viticulture program that would include some of the most advanced techniques of planting, trellising, pruning and harvesting. The Beringer land in Knights Valley, beyond Calistoga, was planted to the best rootstocks suited to the soil and budded to the best varietal clones available. A long-term lease was negotiated with the Gamble family to plant their ranch near Oakville with Cabernet Sauvignon and Chardonnay vines. Next, Beringer staked out and planted Pinot Noir and Chardonnay in a cool micro-climate off Big Ranch Road south of Yountville.

In 1974, Beringer took several steps to upgrade its winemaking facility. The plan was to use the old

The grounds between the Rhine House and the old cellars have

Rhine House, the star of the Beringer visitor center, stands more stately than ever in its completely landscaped setting.

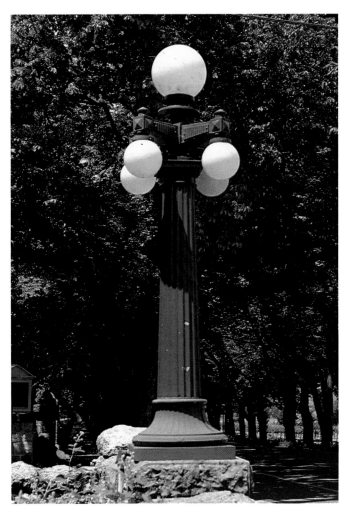

Sentinel to the past. Just as it has for most of this century one of St. Helena's famous street lights, a relic of the 1915 San Francisco Fair, marks the Beringer entrance off the "Tunnel of Elms."

been transformed into a beautifully-planted plaza.

cellars for barrel-aging, while a new state-of-the-art crushing and fermenting facility would go in across the highway, beyond the Tunnel of Elms. The new equipment would be the ultimate for making fine wines, giving the winery the flexibility to hold separate small lots of wine, produce "reserve" and specific vineyard designations, and experiment with special wines.

One of the experiments initiated by Nightingale that held great promise was Chardonnay "barrel-fermented" in French oak. Burgundy winemakers had evolved this labor-intensive process over many decades but only since the 1950s had a small number of California wineries tried the method. It is a style of winemaking that demands attention to detail, and much time and expense, but Nightingale was convinced that it offered the best chance to produce truly world-class Chardonnays. What made the difference was the barrels. American oak just did not impart the character to the wine as did the French Limousin and Nevers barrels.

While the Beringer Chardonnays were gaining a reputation for their elegance and complexity, Nightingale wanted to try out his new winemaking system by making a Private Reserve Cabernet Sauvignon.

The Lemmon Ranch located in a special micro-climate at the base of Glass Mountain about three miles northwest of the winery would supply him with the perfect grapes for the work. This was a well-established vineyard, partly terraced up the hillside, that produced Cabernet Sauvignon bunches with small berries that had intense flavor and deep, rich color. A contract was negotiated for the first of these grapes to be brought in for the 1977 crush.

The '77 Lemmon Ranch Private Reserve Cabernet Sauvignon proved to be the big breakthrough in Beringer quality when, four years later, it won a gold medal at California's Orange County Fair. Widely acclaimed by critics, it was thought by some to be one of the best '77 Cabernets made in the Napa Valley. The 1978 Lemmon Ranch also collected gold medals and suddenly people were paying a lot more attention to the wines made by Beringer.

In at the beginning of this exciting time was young Edward Sbragia who joined Beringer in 1976 as Nightingale's assistant in his experimental winemaking programs. Sbragia, a burly third-generation winemaker whose grandparents settled in the rolling vine-yard country of Healdsburg, had a degree in chemistry from Davis and a master's in enology from Fresno State. Nightingale was so impressed with his early work at Beringer that he would make a point to tell a group of visiting winewriters of the time that . . . "It would be a good idea to keep this young man's name in mind."

Nightingale set high critical standards for Beringer wines and Sbragia would help shape and style them. It was a team that was gaining great respect among wine critics across the nation.

Throughout the increasing popularity of premium wine tastings and competitions it was becoming more obvious that the wineries with the best edge had access to the best grapes. In the Napa Valley where there is a great diversity of conditions, winemakers were making an even greater effort to get the best fruit that the soils, micro-climates and vineyard practices had to offer.

Fortunately, in 1979 Beringer was able to attract one of the top viticulturists in the state to manage its vitally important vineyard operations. Bob Steinhauer held a master's in Plant Science from Fresno State University, among other honors, and lived in St. Helena where he had polished his skills while working several years in the planting and development of several new premium vineyards. Like Nightingale, he was always a step ahead in trying new things to improve on quality.

Steinhauer oversaw the planting of Beringer vineyards with the emphasis on the same quality orientation that Nightingale brought to the winemaking techniques. The right time to pick was critical and he worked closely with the winemaster to deliver grapes with the optimum maturity. One of his major accomplishments was to fully develop the prized Cabernet vineyards in Knights Valley. Other recognition soon came from his work with canopy management and vine budding, which have won him many honors among his peers. In 1985 he was elected President of the American Society of Enology and Viticulture.

Edward Sbragia became Beringer winemaster in 1984, assuming the role from Myron Nightingale who retired as consulting "Winemaster Emeritus." On the death of the pioneer vintner four years later, the winery would honor him by establishing a Nightingale memorial fund for viticulture and enology research at the University of California at Davis.

Meanwhile, Sbragia would advance Beringer wine

The old cellar building rises impressive on the hill above the visitor's plaza.

For many wine fans and novices alike, a tour through the historic Beringer cellars is the most memorable of the Napa Valley.

Today, one of the most visited wineries in Napa Valley, Beringer offers guests a picturesque setting while they queue for the next tour. Each half-hour a trained guide takes a new group through the cellar building and limestone tunnels, explaining the history and how the wine is made and barrel-aged. Pictured at the right is the area of the cellars where most of the wine-making took place from Jacob Beringer's time until the modern facility was built across from the "Tunnel of Elms."

quality another major step by establishing an innovative research program designed, in his words "to get as much as the grape has to offer" in the making of super-premium varietals. To explore all the possibilities of making the very best, he built a research "winery within-the-winery" where a team of assistants carried out controlled studies away from the production facility. Refinements to winemaking and vineyard techniques are accurately assessed and then employed after they have proven to be qualitatively beneficial to the program.

It had long been established that the superior Napa Valley Chardonnays came from the cooler southern regions of the valley and from certain mountain elevations, while the finer Cabernet Sauvignons were grown mostly at mid-valley and on the rocky hillsides with the right soil and exposure. Through the years Beringer had planted carefully and now vineyard master Bob Steinhauer began keeping extensive records on each parcel, and even on individual rows of vines to develop more quality. Steps are taken in the vineyard to improve not only the sugar-acid ratios of the grapes, but to know more precisely when to pick for optimum physiological maturity—rewarding the winemakers with the highest quality of fruit to work with.

By now, demand for the award-winning Beringer wines had become part of a national trend. California premium varietals were soaring in popularity throughout the world and in step with this, Beringer had just completed a new state-of-the-art barrel-aging building. Filled with small French oak barrels, the new "chai" would give the famous old St. Helena cellar additional tools to stay among the Napa Valley's top producers of fine wine. The years of preparation had payed off!

More than one hundred years since its founding, Beringer continues to improve with age. Generations of visitors still come year round to the Rhine House because they think of Beringer as something special. It is. —From the proprietor-grown Chardonnays to the rich, full-bodied Private Reserve Cabernet Sauvignons and the many awards won, the historic old estate has rightfully earned a place among the best names in California wine.

Old Jacob and Frederick Beringer would be pleased to know that the fine cellars and beautiful grounds they established so long ago are still in loving hands and being enjoyed by so many. ≉

Visitors enjoy exploring Rhine House and its gardens. After a tour of the cellars, they can sample some of the wines in the mansion's finely-decorated tasting rooms. Opposite: *Frederick Beringer's spacious bedroom on the second floor has been made into the "Founder's Room." It features hand-carved paneling and a list of Private Reserves for tasting by the more discriminating palates.*

For many, the highlight of Rhine House is a special tasting in the elegant Founder's Room.

A focus on wine and food.

Chef Madeleine Kamman instructs a Beringer class.

Recognized for its culinary programs, Beringer has taken the marriage of fine food and wine a major step forward by establishing The School for American Chefs. Under the direction of internationally recognized chef Madeleine Kamman, the school is located on the winery grounds in Jacob Beringer's old home (Hudson House) which has been rebuilt into a state-of-the-art culinary center. Here, professional chefs and non-chefs can enroll for hands-on classes throughout the year. Born in Paris, Mrs. Kamman is author of six cook books and is the star of PBS-TV's "Madeleine Cooks."

Wine World president Mike Moone with some blue-ribbon chefs at a Beringer dinner. Under his direction the culinary arts have taken a significant role in winery events.

Beringer chefs demonstrate their culinary skills at a dinner hosted in the grand entry hall of the Rhine House.

Wines are sampled before a dinner prepared by twelve Great Women's Chefs is served on the Rhine House lawn. This is just one of the many culinary events presented by Beringer to show the special alliance between fine wine and food.

Over hot coals in the Rhine House gardens, the finishing touches are put on the main-course specialties by the twelve renowned women chefs.

hors d'oeuvres by a chic Chef.

Guests at the Rhine House plaza reception for Beringer's Great Women Chef's dinner.

Vineyard-master Bob Steinhauer has played a key role in the Beringer premium wine success. He works closely with the winemaster to get the optimum quality from each vineyard.

Tying cordoned vines to the trellis wire.

Marolf Vineyard along Silverado Trail in June foliage.

Grapes from here established the now-famous Beringer Zinfandel wines.

Picturesque Bancroft Vineyards at the 2,000-foot level on Howell Mountain grows for Beringer some of the best Cabernet Sauvignon

Connoisseurs and winewriters attending the renowned Napa Valley Wine Auction, held each June, enjoy the spectacular view overlooking St. Helena and the valley from the grounds of Bancroft Vineyards. They were guests at a special Beringer dinner held (below) at Bancroft.

and Merlot in Napa Valley.

The Bancroft summer home overlooking the valley from their vineyards.

Beringer wait staff serves up an outdoor barbecue.

A tent for the dinner, held on the lush Bancroft lawn, wards off the evening alpine chill.

A choice of wines with dinner.

Jim Bancroft (dark suit), and his vineyard manager John Siebel, are pictured with Ed Sbragia, left, and Bob Steinhauer, right. They were the hosts of the special Bancroft wine tasting and dinner sponsored by Beringer for some participants in the annual Napa Valley Wine Auction. Bancroft, whose vineyards high in the Howell Mountain appellation hold great promise, is typical of the independent grower who is part of the Beringer premium wine story.

Beringer winemaster Ed Sbragia and vice-president-winery spokesman Tor Kenward conduct the special tasting of superb wines made from Bancroft Cabernet Sauvignon, Merlot, and Cabernet Franc.

At Beringer, great wines begin with great grapes.

Every year is a good vintage in the Napa Valley. Some are just better than others. Winemakers and growers alike find harvesting the new crop an exciting time, filled with anticipation of another great crush.

The crusher in action.

Inside a stainless fermentation tank. It has been the combination of high-tech winemaking with the old traditions that have made wines produced by Beringer so successful.

Experiments underway

Opposite: *A tank of Cabernet Sauvignon in controlled fermentation.*

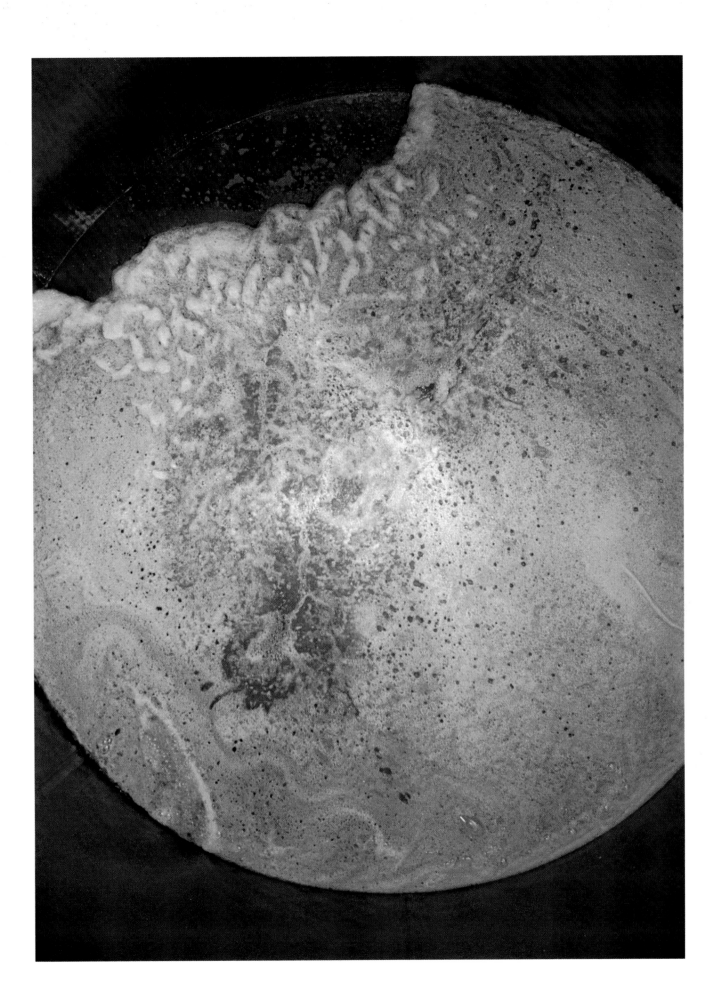

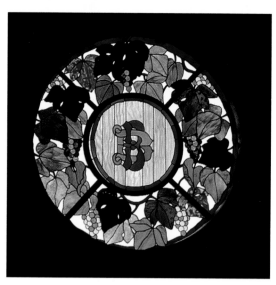

Stained glass "Chai" window.

Designed to blend naturally into the vineyards, the new Beringer barrel-aging building, or "Chai," lies across the road from the old cellars.

A series of "Chai" aging rooms give Beringer the capacity to produce premium wines in a controlled environment. The 55-gallon French oak cooperage is the ultimate for finishing Chardonnay, Cabernet Sauvignon and Fumé Blanc.

Filling French oak with Cabernet Sauvignon in the state-of-the-art Beringer barrel-aging building.

Chef Madeleine Kamman in her new kitchen
at The Hudson House.

Oldest building on the winery grounds, the "Hudson House" has been
transformed into the gracious Beringer Culinary Arts Center.

Jacob Beringer's old family home is now an
architectural masterpiece with spotless kitchens,
inlaid hardwood floors, central cupola, ornate
columns and palladian windows. As the new
culinary center the historic home allows intimate
dining events for guests of the winery.

194

Guests at the premier opening of the Beringer Culinary Arts Center enjoy wine and food in the columned dining room.

The old "Soaked Oak."

Already ancient when it gave shade to the Beringers and their friends more than a century ago, the old "Soaked Oak" is still imposing on the hill behind the Rhine House. A winery legend, it was named by an early tour guide who contrived the story of how the tree grew to such magnificent leaning proportions by secretly tapping with its roots into one of the best barrels of wine stored in the cellar caves. A favorite tale passed on by other guides, the old "Soaked Oak" is one of the most asked-about features of the Beringer tour.

A cast bronze fountain created by acclaimed sculptor Ruth Asawa celebrates Beringer's 112th year in the Napa Valley. Dedicated in 1988 to commemorate the 150th anniversary of the planting of the first Napa Valley grapes, it features historical scenes and figures such as George Yount, the first to plant vines here in 1838, and Jacob and Frederick Beringer, German immigrants who built one of its finest estates and cellars. ❧

Color Photo Credits